MILK AND GALL

by Mathilde Dratwa

Milk and Gall was first performed at Theatre503, London,
on 3 November 2021.

MILK AND GALL

by Mathilde Dratwa

Cast

VERA	**MyAnna Buring**
AMIRA/ANESTHESIOLOGIST	**Sherine Chalhie**
BARBARA/DOCTOR/ELAINE/ HILLARY	**Jenny Galloway**
ALEXA/NANNY/NURSE/ LACTATION CONSULTANT	**Tracy-Anne Green**
MICHAEL/MUELLER	**Matt Whitchurch**

Creative Team

Director	**Lisa Spirling**
Movement Director	**Chi-San Howard**
Designer	**Mona Camille**
Lighting Designer	**Simeon Miller**
Sound Designer	**Roly Botha**
Casting Director	**Amy Blair**
Costume Supervisor	**Malena Arcucci**
Assistant Director	**Daisy Milner**
Associate Movement Director	**Laura Dredger**
Associate Lighting Designer	**Abi Turner**
Vocal and Dialect Coach	**Sarah McGuinness**
Stage Manager	**Rose Hockaday**
Placement Assistant Stage Manager	**Missy Steinbach**
Production Manager	**Zara Janmohamed**
Producer	**Ceri Lothian**
Assistant Producer	**Tian Brown-Sampson**
PR	**Nancy Poole**

CAST

MYANNA BURING – VERA

Theatre includes: *A Very Expensive Poison* (The Old Vic); *The Vote* (Donmar Warehouse); *The Wasp* (Trafalgar Studios); *Strangers on a Train* (Gielgud Theatre); and *Guardians* (Theatre503).

TV Includes: *The Salisbury Poisonings, In the Dark, Downton Abbey, White Heat* (BBC); *The Witcher* (Netflix); and *Ripper Street* (Amazon, BBC TV).

Film includes: *Official Secrets, Hyena, Twilight: Breaking Dawn Parts I & II, Kill List.*

MATT WHITCHURCH – MICHAEL/MUELLER

Matt graduated from RADA in 2014 and since then has worked extensively in television and theatre.

Theatre credits include: *Pine, Labyrinth* (Hampstead Theatre); *The Herbal Bed* (ETT Touring); and *Spiderfly* (Theatre503).

TV credits include: *Call the Midwife, The Outcast* (BBC); and *The Sex Pistols VS. Bill Grundy* (Sky).

JENNY GALLOWAY – BARBARA/DOCTOR/ELAINE/HILLARY

Notable theatre credits includes: *The Welkin, Absolute Hell, After the Dance* (National Theatre); *Starry Messenger* (Wyndham's Theatre); *Mr Foote's Other Leg* (Hampstead and Theatre Royal Haymarket); *Hay Fever* (Noël Coward Theatre); *Anna Christie, How I Learned to Drive, Nine, Electra* (Donmar Warehouse); *Cause Célèbre* (Old Vic); *Madame de Sade* (Donmar at Wyndham's); *Les Misérables* (Palace/Broadway/25th Anniversary at O2); *Mary Poppins* (Prince Edward Theatre and New Amsterdam, New York); *Mamma Mia!* (Olivier Award for Best Performance in a Supporting Role in a Musical; Prince Edward), *My One and Only* (Olivier Nomination for Best Performance in a Supporting Role in a Musical; Piccadilly); *The Boys from Syracuse* (Olivier Award for Best Performance in a Supporting Role in a Musical; Regent's Park) and her solo show *Pirate Jenny* (National Theatre and Triad Theater, New York).

Film credits credits includes: *Come Away, Crooked House, London Road, In Tranzit, About a Boy, The Clandestine Marriage, Frankenstein, Fierce Creatures, Johnny English* and *Little Dorrit.*

Recent television credits includes: *The Queen's Gambit, Good Omens* and *Fleabag.*

SHERINE CHALHIE – AMIRA/ANESTHESIOLOGIST

Sherine Chalhie is a British-born actress, writer and voice-over artist of Syrian and Irish parents. Sherine has written, performed, and produced her solo show *Hijabi Matters* which she performed at Ovalhouse and toured in schools. She is currently adapting the show for TV. She has starred in *Hollyoaks* (Channel 4) and played the female lead of Nicole in the feature film *Terror*. She is a recent graduate of Soho Labs writing program 2021 and is the founder of Shout About it Productions – creating theatre that breaks down cultural stereotypes and empowers women.

TRACY-ANNE GREEN – ALEXA/NANNY/NURSE/LACTATION CONSULTANT

Stage credits include: *Hamlet*, *King Lear* (RSC UK and USA tour); *VV* (Bunker Theatre); *The Taming of the Shrew* (The Arts Theatre); *The New Voice of Home* (Talawa Theatre); *Love is Not Enough* (Kiln Theatre); *Stop Look Listen* (Stephen Joseph Theatre, Theatre503, Edinburgh Festival); *Three Friends* (Courtyard Theatre); *We Are Shadows* (Half Moon Theatre); *Animal Farm* (Broadway Theatre); and *Asylum Monologues* (Ice and Fire Productions).

Television credits include: *Mammals*, *The Power*, *Call the Midwife*, *Gold Digger*, *Prawo Agaty – True Law*, *Miranda* and *Holby City*.

Film credits include: *In Darkness*, *Pusher*, *Pub Monkey*, *Sensation*, *The Novelist* and *Extraordinary Rendition*.

Short-film credits include: *Wings*, *The Act*, *The Hounds Curse* and *Dead Shelter*.

CREATIVE TEAM

MATHILDE DRATWA – WRITER

Mathilde Dratwa's work has been developed and presented by the Ground Floor at Berkeley Rep, Rattlestick, LAByrinth Theater Company, the Great Plains Theater Conference, the Playwrights' Center, and the Young Vic.

Mathilde is a 2021–2024 Core Writer at the Playwrights' Center, a member of Dorset Theater Festival's Women Artists Writing Group, and a two-time Pulitzer Center grant recipient. Recently, she was a Dramatist Guild Foundation Playwriting Fellow, a member of New York Foundation for the Arts' Immigrant Artist Program and a member of the Orchard Project's Greenhouse.

She is currently developing TV shows for Chernin Entertainment, Endeavor Content, Sony TriStar, Red Wagon, Dirty Films, and FX.

Writing credits include: *A Play about David Mamet Writing a Play about Harvey Weinstein*; and *Dirty Laundry* (an Audible commission).

LISA SPIRLING – DIRECTOR

Lisa Spirling is the Artistic Director and Chief Executive of Theatre503 in London. Previously she was the coordinator of the JMK Trust Regional Director's Programme and a founder of Buckle for Dust Theatre Company.

Credits include: *Wolfie, In Event of Moone Disaster* (Theatre503); *Jumpy* (Theatr Clwyd); *Describe the Night, Ken, Pine, Deposit, Fault Lines, I Know How I Feel About Eve* (Hampstead Theatre); *Donkeys' Years, Here* (Rose Theatre); *Hundreds & Thousands* (Buckle for Dust, English Touring Theatre, Soho Theatre); and *Cotton Wool* (Buckle for Dust, Theatre503).

CHI-SAN HOWARD – MOVEMENT DIRECTOR

Movement credits includes: *Typical Girls* (Clean Break, Sheffield Theatres); *Glee and Me* (Royal Exchange); *Just So* (Watermill Theatre); *Home, I'm Darling* (Theatre by the Lake, Bolton Octagon, Stephen Joseph Theatre); *Harm* (Bush Theatre); *Living Newspaper Ed 5* (Royal Court); *Sunnymead Court* (Defibrillator Theatre); *The Effect* (English Theatre Frankfurt); *The Sugar Syndrome* (Orange Tree Theatre); *Oor Wullie* (Dundee Rep/National Tour); *Variations* (Dorfman Theatre, NT Connections); *Skellig* (Nottingham Playhouse); *Under the Umbrella* (Belgrade Theatre, Yellow Earth, Tamasha); *Describe the Night* (Hampstead Theatre); *The Fairytale Revolution, In Event of Moone Disaster* (Theatre503); *Cosmic Scallies* (Royal Exchange Manchester, Graeae); *Moth* (Hope Mill Theatre); *The Curious Case of Benjamin Button, Scarlet, The Tempest* (Southwark Playhouse); and *Adding Machine: A Musical* (Finborough Theatre).

Film credits include: *Hurt by Paradise* (Sulk Youth Films); *Pretending* – Orla Gartland Music Video (Spindle); *I Wonder Why* – Joesef Music Video (Spindle Productions); and *Birds of Paradise* (Pemberton Films).

MONA CAMILLE – DESIGNER

Mona Camille is a graduate of the Architectural Association Interprofessional Studio in London.

Theatre credits include: *The Tree of Objects* (Jackson Lane Theatre); as Associate: *Raya* (Hampstead Theatre); as Assistant: *Death of a Salesman* (Young Vic); and *Summer Rolls* (Park Theatre).

Other credits include: *Cameleonte* (Studio Goodluck, Production Designer); and *The Lost Supper* (Seychelles Biennale of Contemporary Art, Lead Artist).

SIMEON MILLER – LIGHTING DESIGNER

Simeon has worked as a Lighting Designer since he graduated from Mountview Academy in 2010.

He works across theatre, dance, musicals, 'gig theatre' and devised work, and actively contributes to new writing, especially socially and politically conscious work which amplifies oppressed and radical voices.

Selected credits include: *Metamorphoses* (Shakespeare's Globe); *The Mob Reformers* (Lyric Hammersmith); *Subject Mater* (Edinburgh Fringe); *Black Holes* (International Tour); and *High Rise State of Mind* (UK tour).

ROLY BOTHA – SOUND DESIGNER

Roly is a composer and sound designer. They are also an Associate Artist of The PappyShow.

Theatre credits includes: *Fritz & Matlock, Blowhole* (Pleasance); *Broken English* (Bread & Roses); *Tell Me Straight* (King's Head); *Scream Fire, Punk Rock* (Theatre Royal Stratford East); *Helen* (BAC); *Brother* (Southwark Playhouse); *Warheads* (Park Theatre – 2020 Olivier Nominated); *BOYS, GIRLS, CARE* (The PappyShow, touring nationally); and *Making Faitha* (Camden People's Theatre).

Audio credits includes: *It's A Practise Podcast* (The PappyShow); and *Plays For Today, Opening Doors* (Southwark Playhouse).

AMY BLAIR – CASTING DIRECTOR

Amy has been working in casting since 2019, having spent six years previously working as an actress. She has worked in the offices of casting directors including Ginny Schiller CDG and Annelie Powell CDG and is currently casting associate to Anna Kennedy CDG, working across film and TV.

Casting director credits include: *Centralia* R&D (RJG Productions); *Tomboy* (White Bear Theatre); and *My Friend Peter* (UK tour).

Casting consultant credits include: *Roy, An Irish Goodbye* (Floodlight Pictures).

Casting associate credits include: *Meat* (Theatre503, FortyFive North); and *In My Lungs the Ocean Swells* (VAULT Festival).

Background casting director and producer credits include: *Wings* (by Jamie Weston and Carla Fraser).

MALENA ARCUCCI – COSTUME SUPERVISOR

Born and raised in Buenos Aires, Argentina, Malena Arcucci is a performance maker currently based in London. She uses devised and physical theatre techniques, in combination with her background and interest in costume making and sculpture to explore new forms of storytelling. She currently works as a producer and theatre designer, and is co-artistic director of MarianaMalena Theatre Company.

Design credits include: *Friday Night Love Poem* (Zoo Venues Edinburgh); *Point of No Return, La Llorona* (Dance City Newcastle); *The Two of Us* (Theatre Deli); *Playing Latinx* (Camden's People's Theatre); and various productions in Buenos Aires, Argentina.

Associate Designer credits include: *Chiaroscuro* (Bush Theatre); *Thebes Land, Tamburlaine* (Arcola Theatre); and *Dear Elizabeth* (The Gate).

Costume Supervisor and Maker credits include: *The Phantom of the Opera* (Her Majesty's Theatre); *Raya* (Hampstead Theatre); and *Roundelay* (Southwark Playhouse).

DAISY MILNER – ASSISTANT DIRECTOR

Daisy Milner is a director and producer. She is currently also the Associate Producer of Guinness world recording breaking comedy sketch show, NewsRevue and the General Manager & Programmer of the Canal Cafe Theatre. She is a 2020 Theatre Directing MA graduate from Mountview Academy of Theatre Arts.

Directing credits include: *The Other Half Lives* (SpaceUK Edinburgh Fringe, also writer); *Much Ado About Nothing* (Courtyard Theatre); *Baggage* (Spotlight Studios); and *The Thrill of Love* (Mountview Academy).

Assistant Directing credits include: *Mr Burns, Flora the Red Menace* (Mountview Academy).

Producing credits include: *Jimmyville* (SpaceUK Edinburgh Fringe).

LAURA DREDGER – ASSOCIATE MOVEMENT DIRECTOR

Laura Dredger is a freelance movement practitioner, working across the UK. Laura is Founder and Director of MoveSpace, a community organisation that supports and connects Movement Directors, offering CPD opportunities and Creative Learning Director of Yorke Dance Project, a touring contemporary ballet dance company.

Movement Directing credits include: *Julius Caesar, Cymbeline* (LAMDA); *Shakespeare Up Close – Romeo and Juliet, Macbeth* (Orange Tree Theatre); *John Barleycorn Must Die* (Tombola Theatre); *FFF* (Birmingham Rep); *Lysistrata, Twelfth*

Night, *The Wonderful World of Dissocia*, *As You Like It* (Arcola); *My Beautiful City* (National Youth Theatre); *Reach Out Theatre Collective* (Stratford-upon-Avon College); and *The Woods* (Midlands Arts Centre).

Choreography credits include: *Untitled* (The Patrick Centre, The Theatre in the Mill, Midlands Arts Centre); *memattandshell* (The Patrick Centre, The Place); and *inside* (Laban, The Place).

ABI TURNER – ASSOCIATE LIGHTING DESIGNER

Abi Turner is a Lighting and Visual Designer and Director based in South East London. They work in creating diverse, inclusive and accessible theatre and often work on productions that draw attention to the current socio-political climate. Abi graduated with a First Class Honours Degree in Lighting Design from Rose Bruford College in 2020.

Lighting design credits include: *When Rachel Met Fiona* (The Space); *Essentially Black* (Camden People's Theatre); and *The Gut Girls* (Stratford Circus Arts Centre).

Directing credits include: *The Trial of Prince Charming* (Baron's Court Theatre)

Assistant Directing credits include: *The Tragedy of Mariam* (virtual R&D).

ROSE HOCKADAY – STAGE MANAGER

Rose Hockaday graduated from Rose Bruford in 2014 with a degree in Lighting Design, and has since been working as a Freelance Lighting Technician & Stage Manager in London.

Theatre credits include: *Spiderfly*, *Wolfie*, *Art of Gaman* (Theatre503); *You Only Live Forever*, *In Tents and Purposes* (Viscera Theatre); *They Built It. No One Came*, *Jericho Creek* (Fledgling Theatre); *A View from Islington North* (Out of Joint); *The Angry Brigade* (Paines Plough); *Timmy*, *Glitter Punch*, *Sophie, Ben and Other Problems*, *The Festival of Spanish Theatre*, *How to Survive a Post-Truth Apocalypse*, *Lately*, *Antigone*, *Mites*, *Phoenix*, *Pops* and *The Ex-Boyfriend Yard Sale*.

Film credits include: *Heaven Knows*, *Visitors*, *Ignite*, *Pomegranate*, *Wandering Eyes* and *Versions of Us*.

Music videos credits include: *Phase Me Out*, *When You're Gone* and *Saint* (for artist VÉRITÉ).

MISSY STEINBACH – PLACEMENT ASSISTANT STAGE MANAGER

Missy is currently in her final year of studying stage management at the Royal Central School of Speech and Drama.

Stage Management credits include: *Toxic* (Altrincham Garrick Playhouse, Greater Manchester Fringe Festival); *At the Feet of Jesus* (Omnibus Theatre); and *Flux* (Theatre503).

Set Design credits include: *Air Swimming* (The Met Theatre).

ZARA JANMOHAMED – PRODUCTION MANAGER

Zara trained at the Royal Academy of Dramatic Art in Stage and Production Management.

Production Management credits include: *Malindadzimu* (Hampstead Theatre); *Final Farewell* (Tara Theatre); *Fuck You Pay Me, The Process, We Anchor In Hope, Box Clever, Killy Muck, Grotty* (Bunker Theatre); *The Amber Trap* (Theatre503), *Hunger, Hoard, Sitting, Mrs Dalloway* (Arcola Theatre); and *RADA Festival, Dramatic Dining Cabaret* (RADA).

Stage Management credits include: *Dick Whittington and his Cat, 80th Anniversary Gala* (Oxford Playhouse); *A Passage to India* (Tour and Park Theatre); *Raising Martha, Kill Me Now* (Park Theatre); and *Scapegoat* (St Stevens Church).

Other credits include: *Fabric* (Soho and community tour, and at Edinburgh Fringe for Mick Perrin Worldwide).

Theatre503 is at the forefront of identifying and nurturing new voices at the very start of their careers and launching them into the industry. They stage more early career playwrights than any other theatre in the world – with over 120 writers premiered each year from festivals of short pieces to full length productions, resulting in employment for over 1,000 freelance artists through their year-round programme.

Theatre503 provides a diverse pipeline of talent resulting in modern classics like **The Mountaintop** by Katori Hall and **Rotterdam** by Jon Brittain – both Olivier Award winners – to future classics like Yasmin Joseph's **J'Ouvert**, winner of the 2020 James Tait Black Prize and transferred to the West End/BBC Arts and **Wolfie** by Ross Willis, winner of the 2020 Writers Guild Award for Best New Play. Writers who began their creative life at Theatre503 are now writing for the likes of The Crown, Succession, Doctor Who, Killing Eve and Normal People and every single major subsidised theatre in the country now boasts a new play by a writer who started at Theatre503.

THEATRE503 TEAM

Artistic Director	Lisa Spirling
Executive Director	Andrew Shepherd
Literary Manager	Steve Harper
Producer	Ceri Lothian
General Manager	Tash Berg
Carne Associate Director	Jade Lewis
Literary Associate	Lauretta Barrow
Technical Manager	Toby Smith
Administrator	Birungi Kawooya
Trainee Assistant Producers	Tian Brown-Sampson, Hadeel Elshak, Myles Sinclair

THEATRE503 BOARD

Erica Whyman OBE (Chair)
Celine Gagnon (Co-Vice Chair)
Royce Bell (Co-Vice Chair)
Eleanor Lloyd
Emma Rees
Jack Tilbury
Luke Shires
Ollie Raggett
Roy Williams OBE
Sabrina Clarke-Okwubanego
Zena Tuitt

THEATRE503 would like to thank:

Jenna Augen, Stephen Beresford, Alice Birch, Susie Blake, Emily Carewe, Philip Desmeules, Lyn Gardner, Abigail Gonda, Jessica McVay, Solomon Mousley, Charlie Lees-Massey, Kandy Rohmann, Chinonyerem Odimba, Dilek Rose, Alison Steadman, Lauren Stubley, Erica Whyman, Roy Williams and Jessica Woodsford.

OUR SUPPORTERS

We are particularly grateful to Philip and Christine Carne and the long term support of The Carne Trust for our Playwriting Award, the 503 Five and Carne Associate.

Share The Drama Patrons: Angela Hyde-Courtney, Eilene Davidson, Cas & Philip Donald, Erica Whyman, Geraldine Sharpe-Newton, Jack Tilbury/ Plann, Jennifer Jacobs, Jill Segal, Joachim Fleury, Jon and NoraLee Sedmak, Ali Taylor, Tim Roseman, Ian Mill, Jenny Sheridan, Liberty Oberlander, Marcus Markou & Dynamis, Marianne Badrichani, Mike Morfey, Pam Alexander & Roger Booker, Patricia Hamzahee, Richard Bean, Robert O'Dowd, The Bell Family, Sean Winnett and all our 503 Friends and Share The Drama supporters.

The Foyle Foundation, Arts Council England Grants for the Arts, Garrick Charitable Trust, Cockayne Grants for the Arts (503 Productions), Noel Coward Foundation (Rapid Write Response) The Orseis Trust (503Five), Battersea Power Station Foundation (Right to Write), Wimbledon Foundation (Five-O-Fresh), Nick Hern Books (503 Playwriting Award), Wandsworth Borough Council, The Theatres Trust.

Mathilde Dratwa would like to thank:

Jason Wojciechowski, Brian Roff, Amy Fox, Peter Hedges, Kip Fagan, Christina Hodson, Matt Plouffe, Shaharazad Abuel-Ealeh, Ally Shuster, Jen Wineman, Carrie Heitman, Luna Droubi and Zoe Kazan.

MILK AND GALL

Mathilde Dratwa

For my son, who shattered my pretty little life into a thousand little pieces, and then reassembled them into something weird and beautiful, like a Picasso.

And for Paulina, Lola, Aly, Sofia, Rachael, Rachel, Grace, Beverly, Joan, and all the other underpaid workers who care for our children so that we can do other things, like write plays.

Characters

VERA, *thirty-five, a woman who is in labor at the start of the play, gives birth, and therefore subsequently has the body of somebody who has just given birth – including a C-section scar on her abdomen. She is almost always with her shape-shifting baby. American, Jewish, liberal, white, can be unaware of her privilege.*

MICHAEL, *thirties, her husband. Midwestern, white. Deeply loves his wife. Almost always holds a cup of coffee.*

BARBARA, *sixties, her mother. A lesbian. High-energy, a doer.*

AMIRA, *thirties, her best friend. A first-generation Syrian-American. Her friends call her Ami for short, pronounced Ah-mee.*

ALEXA, *thirties, initially a hands-free, voice-controlled device, later a flesh-and-blood mom. Judgemental. Black.*

ELAINE, *Michael's mom. Watches* Fox News. *From Wisconsin, speaks with an accent. Played by Barbara.*

HILLARY CLINTON, *played by Barbara.*

DOCTOR, *played by Barbara.*

MUELLER, *a stereotypical TV detective from a daytime procedural. Played by Michael.*

ANESTHESIOLOGIST, *played by Amira.*

NURSE, *played by Alexa.*

NANNY, *played by Alexa. Speaks with a Caribbean accent.*

LACTATION CONSULTANT, *played by Alexa.*

MOM 1, MOM 2, MOM 3, *played by Alexa, Barbara and Michael.*

Notes

An oblique / indicates where the next character should begin speaking; the dialogue overlaps.

Supertitles can either be projected or spoken aloud by Alexa, the device.

Setting

The play begins in a white, sterile hospital room in New York. As it progresses and moves to Vera and Michael's Brooklyn apartment, more and more stuff is dumped on the set, adding color and chaos. Each new setting is suggested by adding new items. Nothing is ever removed.

Limbo is limbo. It is nowhere.

The park is suggested by trees that appear inside Vera's apartment, and remain inside the apartment after the park scenes as a 'play forest' for the baby.

Finally, the trees become the woods, where Faeries live.

Time and Pacing

The play opens on election night, 2016. The first scene stretches time from November 8, 2016 to November 11, 2016. The play then takes place in the year following that election.

A reminder: that was a fucking relentless year.

The play should be performed in ninety minutes, without an intermission.

There are some specific time references, but generally time bends and blurs and bleeds and sometimes breaks, as it does for most new parents.

The play is fragmented; the form mimics the experience of the sleep-deprived. Vera sleepwalks from scene to scene. She remains in a shocked, tired, on-edge daze until the very last scene, when time finally relaxes, settles, breathes. The baby is suddenly four. (This is how it is in real life: newborn babies are suddenly four. And parents everywhere wonder: how on earth did that happen?)

This text went to press before the end of rehearsals and so may differ slightly from the play as performed.

Supertitle: BIRTH

MICHAEL *and* VERA, *in the hospital. The room is white, pristine, clean.* VERA *is in labor. She has three hospital blankets on her.* MICHAEL *drinks coffee.*

VERA. I'm so cold.

MICHAEL. I'm sorry.

VERA. Are there any more?

MICHAEL. Blankets? I don't think so.

    MICHAEL *takes off his sweater and puts it on her.*

VERA. I don't get it. All this, and I'm shaking. Are you cold?

MICHAEL. No. (*A beat.*) I think it's 'cause your body's in shock. Like when someone dies in a movie? They get cold and shake, too.

VERA. Am I... Am I dying?

MICHAEL. Of course not.

VERA. Why would you fucking say that?

MICHAEL. I just –

VERA. SHUT UP!

    A flood of light, a 'white-up' as opposed to a 'blackout'.

    Things have quickly shifted. VERA *squats, leaning on a chair.* MICHAEL, *in a corner, looks at his phone.*

    VERA *grunts.*

MICHAEL. Sorry.

    A beat. VERA *grunts again. He puts the phone away.*

VERA. Tell me.

MICHAEL. They just called Indiana, Kentucky, and Vermont.

VERA. What – ?

MICHAEL. Vermont for her. Indiana and Kentucky for him.

A contraction:

VERA. No no no no no no –

MICHAEL. Breathe. Breathe.

VERA. What if – she loses?

MICHAEL. She won't. You just have to think about breathing
right now –

VERA. But what if she does?

MICHAEL. She won't.

VERA. Promise?

MICHAEL. I promise.

The NURSE *enters. She connects a machine to* VERA.

NURSE. This is so we can monitor the contractions, and this is
so we can monitor the baby's heartbeat. Did you say you
wanted an epidural or –

VERA. No.

NURSE. Okay. If you change your mind –

VERA. I won't.

NURSE. Okay. I'll be back / in about twenty minutes

VERA (*holding the* NURSE*'s hand for dear life*). Don't leave.
You can't leave me.

NURSE. I will be right back.

She attempts to pry her hand out of VERA*'s. Finally she
exits.*

VERA. I. I. Michael.

MICHAEL. I'm so sorry.

He approaches her. The contraction comes and goes.

VERA. Oh my god.

MICHAEL. You're doing great.

He tries to hold her hand, like the NURSE *just did.*

VERA. DON'T TOUCH ME.

White-up.

The drugs! I want the drugs!

MICHAEL. She's coming. She's going to be here as soon as she can.

VERA. It's like. It's like my bones… are shattering.

MICHAEL. Vee, she's in the ER with a woman who's hemorrhaging.

VERA. I don't care. Let her die. I can't do this.

MICHAEL. Yes you can.

VERA. What – happened? What – states?

MICHAEL. West Virginia and South Carolina. Both for him.

Either because a contraction is starting or because this news makes her unhappy – it's unclear which –

VERA. FUUUUCK!

White-up. A shift. VERA *is not able to talk.* MICHAEL *reads from his phone as she grits her teeth and makes animal sounds.*

MICHAEL. Alabama, Trump. Connecticut, Delaware, Clinton. DC, Clinton. Illinois, Maryland, Massachusetts, Clinton. Mississippi, Trump. New Jersey, Rhode Island, Clinton. Tennessee, Trump. Arkansas, Trump.

White-up. A shift. VERA *sits on the edge of the bed.*

She's here! The anesthesiologist is here, Vee.

The ANESTHESIOLOGIST *enters with a very large needle – and keeps walking, and walking, until the needle is so*

enormous that it fills up the entire room. She sticks it in
VERA*'s back.*

ANESTHESIOLOGIST. I need you to tell me when you feel
    the cold. Not that you feel the contact… But if you feel that
    this is cold. Okay?

The ANESTHESIOLOGIST *moves a piece of gauze around*
VERA*'s thighs.*

Here?

VERA. Yes.

ANESTHESIOLOGIST. Here?

VERA. Yes.

ANESTHESIOLOGIST. Here?

VERA. Yes.

The ANESTHESIOLOGIST *hands her a clicker.*

ANESTHESIOLOGIST. You can press this every fifteen
    minutes. Don't worry about timing it. You can click all you
    want, it's blocked. It won't give you another dose until
    fifteen minutes are up. See?

*Click click click click. Each click is amplified; a distinctive,
non-naturalistic noise.*

VERA. Okay.

White-up. Things have shifted. The ANESTHESIOLOGIST
disappears. VERA *lies on the bed.*

MICHAEL. Okay. He got Kansas,

She clicks. The click is loud, distinctive, amplified.

Louisiana,

She clicks.

Nebraska,

She clicks.

The Dakotas,

Click, click.

Texas,

Click.

Wyoming,

Click.

She got New York.

White-up.

The DOCTOR *and* NURSE *stand by the bed.*

DOCTOR. Okay, it's time to push. You can't click anymore, it's disconnected.

The NURSE *pries the clicker from her hand.*

You have to focus. Okay? Did they teach you how to push?

VERA *looks blankly at the* DOCTOR.

Do you know if you prefer to hold your breath and push, or slowly exhale as you push? Did they go over that? In your birthing class?

VERA. We didn't… We were going to…

MICHAEL. We were planning on doing that next week. This is a month early. We thought we had more time.

NURSE. That's exactly why you start preparing early. With a geriatric pregnancy, there's no such thing as overprepared. (*A beat.*) You can take a deep breath and then hold it, and push, like this – (*Demonstrates.*) Or you blow as you push. Softly. Like this – pffffffffffff – (*Demonstrates.*) Do you want to try them both? See which one you like best?

VERA *tries them both.*

VERA. I think I like the blowing one.

NURSE. Great. Fantastic.

DOCTOR. Baby's coming nicely. Four big pushes and we'll be done here.

NURSE. When you feel a contraction coming, that's when you take a breath, then push through the contraction.

VERA. Okay.

Everyone gets into position. VERA pushes. She pushes again. And again. She starts to make a low, sustained grunt – and looks to the NURSE and DOCTOR for help. Head down, both the DOCTOR and NURSE are checking their phones. Her grunt abruptly stops, as –

Ohio –

DOCTOR. Florida –

NURSE. It looks like Pennsylvania –

DOCTOR. The numbers from Wisconsin –

VERA. What do you mean Wisc– ? (*To MICHAEL.*) Wisconsin?! Wisconsin?! That's on you.

NURSE. Just push, please.

VERA. Did they call it yet?

NURSE. You have to focus. The baby's heart rate –

VERA. Did she win?

MICHAEL. Ummm…

NURSE. Okay. Here comes the head –

MICHAEL. Oh my god. A head.

VERA. Did? Did?

NURSE. Push, please.

VERA pushes. Pfffffffffff.

Harder.

VERA pushes. Pfffffffffff.

DOCTOR. Oh no. Shoulder dystocia –

MICHAEL. Oh no? What do you mean 'oh no'? What's /
    shoul–

NURSE. The baby's shoulder is wedged in the pelvis.

DOCTOR (*to* MICHAEL). Sir? You're going to have to / step
    back.

MICHAEL. But –

NURSE. The concern is the lack of oxygen to the baby. Birth
    asphyxia.

DOCTOR. Sir? Step back please.

NURSE. The contractions can cause intense pressure that can
    compress the cord, cutting off the connection to the baby.

MICHAEL. Vee –

NURSE. The baby is at risk of permanent nerve damage, which
    may include brachial plexus or Erb's palsy. Or fetal demise.

VERA. What?

DOCTOR. Let's try the McRoberts maneuver.

NURSE. Ma'am? We need you to bend your legs to your chest.

    VERA *grunts*.

DOCTOR. Don't push.

VERA. What?

NURSE. Do not push.

    The DOCTOR *and* NURSE *try the McRoberts maneuver. No
    luck.*

MICHAEL. What are you doing?

NURSE. I'm applying suprapubic pressure. Pushing on the
    stomach at a forty-five-degree angle, to rotate and push the
    trapped shoulder below the pubic bone. Push. Push.

DOCTOR (*urgently, to the* NURSE). Surgical scissors, please.

NURSE (*quickly passing them to the* DOCTOR). Surgical scissors.

VERA. What's... Happening?

NURSE. Episiotomy. Some doctors believe that a cut between the vagina and anus can increase the amount of room for delivery.

VERA. But –

DOCTOR. It's going to be the Zavenelli maneuver.

NURSE (*to* MICHAEL). Sir? You're going to have to step back.

VERA. What's happening?

NURSE (*to* MICHAEL). Sir? NOW.

MICHAEL. What's a Zava– ?

NURSE. We're going to push the baby back in.

VERA. WHAT?

NURSE. We're going to place the baby back into the vagina, and then perform an emergency C-section.

Very quickly, the NURSE *sets up a curtain for the C-section, blocking* VERA*'s lower half.*

VERA. I don't understand –

NURSE. There are signs of fetal distress.

DOCTOR. We can't waste any time.

VERA. What? What's going on? I'm freaking out. Michael? Tell me what's happening!

MICHAEL unintentionally looks at what's going on behind the curtain. It's horrific. He'll never get that sight out of his brain.

MICHAEL. Um...

Everyone freezes.

She won. Hillary won.

The DOCTOR *and* NURSE *look at each other, puzzled. Then look at their phones. And back at* MICHAEL – *that's gonna go badly…*

White-up. This one lasts longer.

Morning. The delivery room has transformed into a hospital room.

MICHAEL *drinks coffee.* VERA *lies in one of the two beds. The baby is very delicate, made of glass. It is in a bassinet.*

Vee, about last / night

VERA. Did he call her to concede?

MICHAEL. Uh – no –

VERA. Fucker. You *always* call to concede.

MICHAEL. There's something I need to tell –

The door opens gently. AMIRA *enters. She has not slept all night, and has been crying.*

AMIRA. Oh Vee – how are you?

She rushes to her friend. MICHAEL *tries to catch her eye.* VERA *flinches as* AMIRA *hugs her.*

Sorry! Shit –

VERA. It's okay –

AMIRA. The nurse outside said something about –

VERA. I'm fine.

MICHAEL. She's –

VERA. I'm fine.

A beat.

AMIRA. At least the baby's healthy.

VERA. Right.

AMIRA. You look amazing. Considering you almost died.

VERA. You look like shit.

MICHAEL (*apologizing for* VERA). The hormones.

AMIRA. No, it's okay, I know. I haven't slept... Oh my god, oh my god, look at him.

MICHAEL (*trying to catch her eye*). Hey, Amira?

AMIRA. This, right here, this little dude, this amazing little superdude is literally the best thing, because I swear if it wasn't for –

MICHAEL (*loudly, interrupting her*). Do you want to hold him?

AMIRA. Can I? I would love to. Hi there, Superdude. It's nice to meet you.

She holds the glass baby.

(*To* VERA.) So did you poop on the delivery table?

VERA. You bet your ass I did.

They laugh. BARBARA *opens the door, dramatically, and enters. She rushes to her daughter.*

BARBARA. Oh honey!

VERA. Hi, Mom.

BARBARA. I got here as fast as I could – How are you? How was the delivery?

VERA. I'm fine.

BARBARA (*to* MICHAEL *and* AMIRA). How is she?

MICHAEL. She has something called puerperal sepsis.

AMIRA. Is that –

MICHAEL. It's fairly common after a C-section, apparently. She needs to rest, and, uh, it's important to avoid any type of stress, so –

BARBARA. Well – at least the baby's healthy. Right?

VERA. I just wish it was a girl. You know? That would be so badass. To give birth to a girl on a day like this.

MICHAEL (*clearing his throat*). Vera's very excited that she gave birth on the same day that America elected the first woman president.

BARBARA and AMIRA look at MICHAEL, then at each other. A beat: they understand the situation. Another beat: they make a decision, collectively. They begin speaking, too fast, at the same time.

AMIRA. A / boy is great. A boy is great too.

BARBARA. This is definitely a unique day. Not like any other day.

VERA. Did they let you bring in your phones? Michael said they won't let us have ours in here. Even though the doctor and nurse were on their phones *during my delivery.* Can you believe it? How are we supposed to take pictures?

A beat.

MICHAEL. Barbara, do you want to hold the baby?

BARBARA. The baby! Oh my gosh. Of course. Yes. What's his name?

VERA. We can't decide. It's either going to be Clint –

BARBARA. Like Eastwood?

VERA. Like the *president.* Or Rod. I like the sound of Clint better but you know, Clint, Clinton, that could point to Bill, too, and fuck Bill. So I think Rod is actually a more profound decision.

AMIRA. How does Bernie Bro over here feel about that?

MICHAEL. We're going to take a few days to think about it.

White-up. A bigger bend in time.

The night of November 9 to November 10. MICHAEL and AMIRA disappear. A figure tiptoes around VERA's hospital

room while she sleeps: BARBARA *is transforming into*
ELAINE, *who is more heavyset, and wears more feminine*
clothes and speaks with a Wisconsin accent. VERA *wakes up*
and grabs the closest object – a hairbrush.

VERA. Get away from my baby! Get away from my baby! I'll
cut you! HELP! HELP!

ELAINE. Honey, honey, I'm sorry, I didn't mean to wake you.
It's me. It's just me. Elaine.

She switches on the light.

VERA. Oh. I'm sorry. I thought you were a baby-snatcher.
Apparently that's a thing. They showed us a video in the
recovery room – they said to beware of any woman roaming
the hospital –

ELAINE. My flight was delayed. I wanted to come straight
here… I'm sorry. I didn't think it through. You must be worn
slap out, honey.

VERA. That's okay.

ELAINE. I heard it was a toughie. But, at least the baby's
healthy. Right?

She sees the glass baby.

Oh and dere he is. Would you look at that. My first grandson.
Why hello dere, poopie pie. You know, dere were times, with
Michael, when I thought dis day would never come.

VERA. I / know

ELAINE. He used to say he'd never have kids, after his dad left.

VERA. I know –

ELAINE. And everyone else is on baby number three or four –
his friends, his cousins, but not my Mikey – (*Shakes her*
head.) bless his heart. Mikey Anderson likes to take his time.

VERA. He's not *behind*, here. We're actually the first. Of our
friends, to have a baby.

ELAINE. Oh, sure.

A beat.

Are you going to have / another one?

VERA. I should get Michael –

She sits up in bed, lets out a little cry and holds her abdomen – she is in pain.

ELAINE. I'll get him, honey. You lie down. Where is he?

VERA. Sleeping on a bench in the hallway. He couldn't get comfortable on the chair so –

ELAINE (*motioning to the second bed*). But what / about

VERA. Oh, he's not allowed on there. We didn't pay for a private room.

ELAINE. But nobody's in it! I don't understand how the two of you can / live in –

VERA. We love it here.

A beat.

ELAINE. Well sure, honey. As long as you're happy.

VERA. Do you want to hold the baby?

ELAINE. Oh gosh. Could I?

VERA. He's your grandson.

She hands ELAINE *the glass baby.*

ELAINE. Aren't you a cutie patootie. Little doodlebug. He still doesn't have a name?

VERA. We're not a hundred percent yet. But I'm leaning towards Rod.

ELAINE. Rod?

VERA. Yeah. Rod. Roddy. For Rodham.

ELAINE. Oh, honey. You can't name him after her. I know we don't see eye to eye, but... You cannot name my grandson after a murderer. She killed people. She actually –

VERA. Elaine, I don't want to fight. Not now.

ELAINE. I would have liked a female president too, you know. Just not *dat* one. Bernie would have been okay. I agree with Michael on dat one. But her? She's going to jail.

VERA (*sighing*). I'm sorry… I'm trying. Because you're my son's grandma. But Trump is a fucking / prick

ELAINE. Vera, hush your mouth! The baby!

VERA. Oh, the baby's a baby. He doesn't know what prick means.

VERA *takes the baby back.*

Come on, Elaine. I can't say prick but he can grab pussies?

ELAINE. He's not polished, I'll give / you dat

VERA. He stands for racism and sexism and, and – all the isms. Do you realize what it would have done to this country if he'd won?

ELAINE*'s jaw drops – and keeps dropping. She keeps trying to interrupt* VERA *during this speech, but* VERA*'s on a roll and doesn't even pause.*

It would have ripped it apart. This election wasn't about Democrat or Republican, Elaine. This election was about – do we want to be *mean*, or not.

ELAINE. / But

VERA. And so this is a pretty historic time,

ELAINE. / But

VERA. and I'm gonna name my son whatever the fuck I want to name him. 'Cause I can.

ELAINE. But, honey? She lost.

A beat.

VERA. What?

ELAINE. She lost. He won. I don't know what they told you, but. (*Somewhat triumphantly.*) He won.

VERA *drops the baby. Made of glass, it shatters on the floor. White-up.*

During the transition, ELAINE *disappears,* MICHAEL *enters, and* VERA *screams. The scream seems to last forever; it is full of rage and venom and desperation. It's an animal scream; it comes from her gut.*

MICHAEL *gathers the pieces of glass, putting them into a pillowcase.*

VERA. Aaaaaaaaaaaaaaaaaaaaaaaaaaaaaaaaaaaaaahhhhhhhhhhhhhh hhhhhhhhhhhhhh

A beat as she catches her breath.

Aaaaaaaaaaaaaaaaaaaaaaaaaaaaaaaaaaaaahhhhhhhhhhhhhhhhhhh hhhhhhhhhh

MICHAEL. I'm sorr–

VERA *flings herself at him as best she can – she's still in pain.*

VERA. You son of a bitch piece of shit lying motherfucking asshole.

He tries to hold her. She beats his chest.

MICHAEL. Vee, you were going through so much. I was just trying to protec–

VERA *swings at him.*

VERA. To *protect* me?

MICHAEL. You were in the middle of *giving birth*. And things were going wrong. And I couldn't stop the pain. I couldn't make you warm. This was the one thing I could / do

VERA. It's not *about* you –

MICHAEL. It was a – I thought it was – an act of kindness –

VERA. Of / *kindness*? You *lied* to me

MICHAEL. I just wanted to give you –

VERA. What? What the fuck did you give me?

MICHAEL. A day. I gave you a day.

A beat. Very slowly, she turns to the baby: now a pillowcase filled with shattered glass. She whispers.

VERA. I'm sorry. I'm sorry. I'm sorry. I'm sorry. I'm sorry.

A beat.

(*Breaking.*) If I had known... If I had known this is where we were going – (*Touches the baby.*) I wouldn't have had you.

VERA *stands by the window, spent, cradling the pillowcase filled with shattered glass.* MICHAEL *packs their bag. The* NURSE *enters with a wheelchair.*

NURSE. All set?

A beat. VERA *doesn't respond.*

MICHAEL. Uh – yeah. Thanks.

Slowly, VERA *turns towards them.*

NURSE. How was the night? Did he sleep through?

A beat. VERA *doesn't respond.*

I have some papers for you guys to sign –

MICHAEL *reads and signs the papers.* VERA *signs the papers without reading them.*

I have to ask – have you used the bathroom yet? For a number two? Because I can't let you leave unless you've gone to the bathroom.

VERA *grunts.*

Was that a yes? I'm sorry. I need a verbal yes.

VERA. Yes.

NURSE. Okay, then!

The NURSE *motions towards the wheelchair.*

Your ride.

VERA. I can walk.

NURSE. It's standard procedure. You have to –

VERA. I can walk.

NURSE. I'm really sorry. It's a legal / thing

VERA (*demonstrates walking. She gets louder and louder until she is shouting*). I. Can. Walk. Look at me I'm walking look at me I am fucking walking fuck this I can walk damn it I can walk.

The truth is, she can barely walk.

NURSE. Please, I'm just tryna help –

VERA. But I don't need it. I. Don't. Need. It. I'm not disabled. I don't – have a disability. I have a *baby*.

MICHAEL (*appalled at the way she's treating the* NURSE). Vee, stop it. She needs you to sit. It's her job.

Deflated, she sits in the wheelchair, holding her pillowcase-baby. MICHAEL *exits with the bags. The* NURSE *follows, wheeling* VERA *towards the door.*

The hospital gives way to VERA *and* MICHAEL*'s apartment. In the half-light,* VERA *hands the baby to* MICHAEL*, who walks with it, soothing it. The wheelchair disappears as he hands the baby back to her. It is now her turn to walk and soothe it.* MICHAEL *pours coffee from a coffee-maker to a Thermos.*

Supertitle: TALK TO YOUR BABY (PART 1)

MICHAEL *picks up a messenger bag and sips coffee from his Thermos.*

MICHAEL. Are you sure you're gonna be okay?

VERA. *Yes.*

MICHAEL. Call me if there's anything – anything at all – okay?

VERA. *Okay.*

He blows a kiss in her general direction, and goes to work, leaving her on the sofa, holding the pillowcase-baby. The loose ends of the pillowcase are now tied; the baby is shaped like a large egg; it's on its way to becoming a tiny little bit more human. The door closes – not quite a slam, but not quite gently, either.

Long pause.

She looks at her pillowcase-baby. Another pause.

Hi.

The baby does not react. She tries to think of something to say.

Hello.

This is hard. She raises her voice to speak to ALEXA, *the voice-controlled, hands-free Amazon Echo Dot on the table.*

Alexa.

ALEXA *flashes on.*

What should I say to my baby?

ALEXA, THE DEVICE (*monotone*). I did not understand the question I heard.

VERA. Alexa.

ALEXA *flashes again.*

What does one talk about with a baby – to a baby?

ALEXA, THE DEVICE. Talking is important for building your baby's brain. In the first three years of life, your baby's brain triples in size.

VERA. Fuck. / That's crazy.

ALEXA, THE DEVICE. Try giving your baby a 'play-by-play', narrating what you are doing as you change her diaper, or describing what you see as you take her for a walk.

VERA. Alexa. My baby's a boy.

ALEXA, THE DEVICE. I did not understand the question I heard.

VERA. Why does everyone use 'she'? Not all babies are girls!

Short beat.

(*To herself.*) Maybe that's not a very feminist thing to say.

Longer beat. She stands and points out objects around the room, showing the baby furniture. As she stands, it becomes obvious that, under her T-shirt, she wears nothing but mesh underwear stolen from the hospital. The mesh underwear holds a maxi-pad in her crotch. (A home-made padsicle; look it up.)

Chair. Table. Sofa. Stupid sign –

She pulls angrily at a sign in the window – an 'I'm with Her' sign that was facing the street. She tosses it away under a bookcase.

Chair. Window. Broken lamp.

She's at a loss again.

Chair.

VERA *looks out of the window. And keeps looking… And looking.*

Supertitle: MONDAY-NIGHT FOOTBALL

MICHAEL *returns home from work and finds* VERA *in exactly the same position he left her.*

MICHAEL. Hey, my loves.

VERA *mumbles a response.*

You okay?

VERA. Mmm.

MICHAEL. What did you do all day?

VERA *gives him a LOOK.*

What?

VERA. I didn't – I –

MICHAEL. What? What is it?

VERA. I literally don't know what to say to him. He's gonna be really dumb and it's all my fault.

MICHAEL. What are you talking about?

VERA. If you don't talk to a baby and expose them to a lot of new words they end up dumb.

MICHAEL. Says who?

VERA. Alexa.

ALEXA *flashes on at the mention of her name, listening for a question.*

But I don't know how to talk to him – (*She's talking fast because she's upset.*) I tried. I swear. / But it feels so weird –

ALEXA, THE DEVICE. I did not understand the question I heard.

VERA. Alexa, fuck you.

ALEXA, THE DEVICE. That's not very nice to say.

VERA. I hate her.

MICHAEL. She's not a real person.

VERA. I still hate her.

MICHAEL *touches* VERA.

MICHAEL. We can figure it out.

VERA. Maybe you can, but I can't. You're supposed to just say out loud all the things you're doing, like a 'play-by-play', but I am not doing anything. I told him. 'I'm sitting here not doing anything.' And then I was done. I had nothing.

MICHAEL. A play-by-play? (*A beat.*) Come here.

MICHAEL *takes the baby from* VERA. *He starts running around the apartment with the pillowcase, holding it like a football.*

Interception by Michael Roth-Anderson! There he goes up the middle, twenty-five, cuts it outside, thirty, forty...

VERA *is trying very hard to look Not Amused.*

– to the fifty, to the forty, to the thirty –

VERA *slowly gets up and grabs the pillowcase-baby from him, because That's Enough.*

Handing off to Vera Anderson-Roth –

She gives him a Look.

There she goes towards the end zone, look at her go –

She can't help it. She smiles. And then she takes off and fakes left but goes right...

Oh my goodness she's still going! And Vera Roth-Anderson is going all the way!! Touchdownnnnn!!!!!

VERA *touches the pillowcase-baby to the ground.*

Holy cow! They're storming the field!! Here they come!!

MICHAEL *begins doing a celebratory dance – he's out of shape and looks silly but he's having fun – and so is she.*

She joins in the dance as they toss the pillowcase baby *and forth.*

Alexa. Play 'We Are The Champions'.

She does. And VERA *holds the pillowcase-baby above her head like a trophy.* MICHAEL *kisses him, maybe like a trophy, or maybe just like a baby.*

NG HOUR

d baby cries. A lot. It is loud. VERA *walks
one wall to another attempting to soothe
ugh space. She switches to a circle – a
artment is small – and alternately bounces*

VERA. Shhhhh. Shhhhh. Shhhhh.

*The baby continues to cry. The sound of the upstairs
neighbors waking up above. Footsteps, doors.*

(*Glancing up.*) Shit. Go to sleep, little man. Go to sleep. Or,
just – can you cry a little quieter?

The baby cries louder. Banging from the ceiling: the neighbors.

VERA *keeps walking/rocking/bouncing. She tries putting the
baby face-down on her forearm. That calms him a little.
Finally the cries become like hiccups. They stop right as*
VERA *sits on the sofa and the light changes to something
not quite naturalistic. The baby is asleep.* VERA *lets her
head fall back on the sofa with relief. A moment passes.*

VERA *lifts her head back up. She sees a book on the coffee
table. Epic music begins to play as she reaches for the book
in slow motion, trying not to wake the baby. She tries various
body contortions before giving up.*

*On the sofa – just out of reach – she sees the TV remote. As
the music swells, she tries to get the remote. Every time she
gets close, the remote moves away from her. She tries to grab
it with her toes, but again, it slips further away. As if by
magic, it lifts off the sofa and floats in mid-air. Various
objects lift up into the air and hover around the room: a
computer, an iPad, books, food, drinks, a cell phone.*

The door to the bedroom opens and MICHAEL *pokes his
head out.*

MICHAEL. Vee?

*The music stops abruptly and all the objects come crashing
to the floor.*

Supertitle: LOVE

Daybreak. VERA *is in the same spot, looking like she hasn't slept (she hasn't).* MICHAEL *enters and opens the blinds, chatting as he does so.*

MICHAEL. Hey, do you think... Are we supposed to send out thank-you cards? I feel like we should. Right? 'Cause I was thinking we could do Paperless? I could do it. At work. If you just give me the email addresses of –

He notices that she's contorting in a strange position.

Vee?

VERA *clutches her abdomen.* MICHAEL *kneels next to her.*

Hey. Hey. Vee?

VERA. Don't.

MICHAEL. Don't what?

VERA. Don't ask.

MICHAEL. Are you okay?

A beat.

Should I call a doctor?

VERA. No. I'm fine.

MICHAEL. Okay, you're clearly not fine –

VERA. Don't. You fucking. Tell me what I –

MICHAEL. I'm gonna call a doctor.

VERA. No!

MICHAEL *(touching her back).* What is it?

She swats his arm away.

Are you in labor? Is there another one coming? Because this is exactly what you / were like

VERA. Very funny.

MICHAEL. Tell me.

VERA. I don't want to go.

MICHAEL. Where?

VERA. 'Go.' (*A beat.*) To the bathroom.

MICHAEL. Uh, okay.

VERA. But I / have to

MICHAEL. So what's / the

VERA. Take a shit.

MICHAEL. Oh.

VERA. Mike, I can't. I really can't. There's stitches down there and it's all ripped up and just the tiniest pressure hurts so bad –

MICHAEL. But at the hospital you said –

VERA. I lied.

A beat.

MICHAEL. Come on.

VERA. I'm scared.

MICHAEL. I'll go with you.

VERA. I don't want you to / go with me.

MICHAEL. Okay, so I'll wait outside.

He puts the pillowcase-baby into the bassinet, then lifts
VERA *up and places a hand on her back. He leads her to the bathroom.*

VERA. Ow. Ow. Ow. Ow. Ow. Ow.

MICHAEL. I think they said – if you raise your legs?

VERA. I changed my mind. Can you come in here?

He goes in.

I don't wanna I don't wanna I don't wanna.

MICHAEL. You have to.

VERA. This sucks.

MICHAEL. It's gonna be okay. Just relax.

VERA. Fuck you.

MICHAEL. I love you.

VERA. I love you.

   She poops.

Supertitle: THE LACTATION CONSULTANT

MICHAEL *has disappeared.* VERA *attempts to breastfeed her baby. She bites down on her fist, clearly in pain. The* LACTATION CONSULTANT *speaks in measured tones, with a permanent smile.*

LACTATION CONSULTANT. Let's try the cross cradle hold, here –

She gently repositions the baby, which is still a large egg-shaped pillowcase, tied at the end.

You hold him with your other hand, like this – it feels counter-intuitive, I know. Tummy-to-tummy, like / this

VERA. Is it supposed to feel like someone is slicing my nipples with glass?

LACTATION CONSULTANT. He needs to learn to latch correctly, that's / all

VERA. But he doesn't / want to

LACTATION CONSULTANT. Try to rub the nipple around his mouth first, then if you aim for the top of his mouth. See if you can keep him awake –

VERA. Look, munchkin, it's a boob. A boobie. I'm rubbing it all over your face. See? Niiippple. Niiiple. Can you smell it? Munchkin? Stay awake, munch, you gotta stay awake. Come on, look at me, look at me –

LACTATION CONSULTANT. Sometimes if you tickle their feet –

VERA (*tickling his foot*). Come on, come on –

LACTATION CONSULTANT. Let's take a break.

She gently takes the baby.

How did the delivery go?

VERA. Not good.

LACTATION CONSULTANT. Sometimes that can be it. A traumatic birth can stunt milk production. Have you tried hand-expressing, just to –

VERA. I can't get anything / out

LACTATION CONSULTANT. Here, let's try again –

She puts the baby in the bassinet and tries to help VERA *hand-express some breastmilk. It's painful and uncomfortable for* VERA.

VERA. I thought *birth* was supposed to be the hardest part.

LACTATION CONSULTANT. There we go, see? There's a little bit –

VERA. Can we go back to / the baby

LACTATION CONSULTANT. I have to be honest with you. All babies lose weight at the very beginning, that's normal. But by now he should be gaining six ounces a week.

VERA (*upset*). What are you / saying?

LACTATION CONSULTANT. I recommend, at this point I recommend giving him some supplements / to make sure he doesn't

VERA. Do you mean formula?

LACTATION CONSULTANT. Formula, yes / because if

VERA. I just, that's not what I –

LACTATION CONSULTANT. It's dangerous for him to be losing weight like this at this stage.

During the following lines spoken by the LACTATION CONSULTANT, *the baby begins to float up, up, up, out of the bassinet and out of sight.*

Is he sleeping through the night?

VERA. I don't know. He sleeps for – I guess the biggest chunk is maybe five hours?

LACTATION CONSULTANT. You're going to have to wake him to feed him. Every three hours.

VERA. Ok/ay

LACTATION CONSULTANT. He needs to start packing on the pounds, and quick. Because there are some serious risks associated with weight loss in infants...

The LACTATION CONSULTANT *disappears.*

Supertitle: FAILURE TO THRIVE

MICHAEL *comes home holding a cup of coffee.* VERA *thrusts a pack of formula in* MICHAEL*'s face. During the scene, the pillowcase-baby slowly sinks back down, like a deflated balloon. There's nothing that looks quite so sad as a deflated balloon.*

VERA. Failure to thrive. Can you believe they seriously call it that? Did they have a competition to come up with the meanest, most fucked-up name for it?

MICHAEL. What?

VERA. You have to make this. Right now.

MICHAEL. Vee, calm / down

VERA. They fail to gain weight appropriately and they can essentially die.

MICHAEL. Vee –

VERA. So you have to make this.

MICHAEL. Okay –

VERA. Like, right now.

MICHAEL. Okay, I'll go in a minute, okay? Just give me –

VERA. No. Right now.

MICHAEL. I don't even know / how

VERA. Here. The instructions are right here. There's a scoopy thing. A measure. You mix it with water. And warm it up.

MICHAEL. Okay, okay.

VERA. It's not rocket science.

MICHAEL. Why do I have to –

VERA. Because I couldn't. Okay? I couldn't bring myself to. But. From now on. We have to – basically we set an alarm for every three hours, and I do fifteen minutes on each breast, and we try to keep him awake and get him to latch, and then right after that I pump for fifteen minutes to try and increase milk supply, and while I pump, you feed him the formula, out of the cap of the bottle, to avoid nipple confusion, because apparently they can just sip from a / cup and

MICHAEL. Nipple confusion? Seriously? That's a thing? Like, 'I'm confused, what is this' –

He goes for her breast. VERA *smacks his hand away. It is more violent than either of them expected.*

VERA. Can you please make the goddamn formula?

MICHAEL *gives her a look, then snatches the formula from her.*

Supertitle: SPILLED MILK

MICHAEL *is cup-feeding the deflated pillowcase-baby while*
VERA *pumps.*

BARBARA *is gawking at the cup-feeding.*

BARBARA. That's incredible.

> MICHAEL *nods.* VERA *turns her head away from her*
> *mother, a little stung.*

I've just never seen a baby drink from a cup like that –

VERA. It's not a cup. It's the top of a bottle.

BARBARA. It's incredible.

VERA. You said that already.

BARBARA. Honey, I've just never seen anything / like it
before

VERA. I got it, Mom. Okay? I got it.

> *A beat.*

BARBARA. And so you do this, you give him this cup of
formula each time? After each –

VERA. That's not formula.

BARBARA. Oh –

VERA. That's breastmilk.

BARBARA. But I thought –

VERA. We collect it, each time I pump, every three hours, and
we keep whatever we get, and keep adding to it, and then
when we get enough –

BARBARA. Oh, well that's great, isn't it, that's what you
wanted, that's gr–

VERA. Well, that's, like, two whole days' worth of pumping
right there, so –

BARBARA. Tell me again how it works?

VERA. There's nothing to tell. He just drinks, Mom. How does it work when you drink?

BARBARA. I mean, the part about why he, about how it's better than a bottle?

MICHAEL (*trying to be helpful*). The mechanism, the way they lap from a cup, it's actually the same movement as from a br– (*Starts to say 'breast' – and to indicate a breast with his hand – and catches himself.*) as, uh, when they're / nursing

VERA. Breastfeeding –

BARBARA. It's just so fascinating –

As she speaks, BARBARA leans in to look more closely at the baby feeding. MICHAEL, who hadn't seen her coming, shifts in his seat and the cup goes flying, spilling the breast milk on the carpet. For a moment everything is still.

(*Trying to relieve the tension.*) Well, you know what they say, there's no use crying over –

VERA makes an animal sound.

MICHAEL and BARBARA disappear.

Supertitle: TALK TO YOUR BABY (PART 2)

It is a few weeks later. VERA *sits, mostly naked, her legs spread around a mirror. By this point, she is very good at Talking to the Baby. The pillowcase is beginning to look more substantial as it gains weight. She talks to the pillowcase-baby as she tries to look in between her legs.*

VERA. Facebook must know that I just gave birth, because I keep getting these ads for transvaginal mesh. Transvaginal mesh is this thing that you implant in your vagina to prevent your bladder, uterus or rectum from literally falling out of it. Which is terrifying. So now I'm surveying the damage. To my vagina.

Vagina. Can you say vagina? Nope, of course not, because you can't say shit.

It would be funny if that were your first word though. Va-Gi-Na. Maybe I'll keep teaching it to you and you can freak your dad out when you turn one or two or however old babies are when they start talking, and say vagina.

Alexa. When do babies start talking?

ALEXA, THE DEVICE. Babies usually say their first word between ten and twelve months, but don't speak in sentences until they are about twenty months or older.

VERA (*to the baby*). Va-Gi-Na. Va-Gi-Na. You have a penis. Pe-Nis. This is different. This is what you'll be sticking your penis into one day. I mean, not mine, that would be very, very, very wrong. But someone else's. If you're into that. It's okay if you're not. You can also stick it other places.

When you came out, you got stuck in there. So then they took you out of *here* – (*Pointing to her scar.*) and at first, you were kind of grey. Not for long, just for a few seconds. They put you against my chest, they call it skin-to-skin, and you turned pink pretty fast.

Supertitle: SEX

VERA *is suddenly – magically – wearing a full cow costume
with the pillowcase-baby connected to her – it dangles from the
udders. She sits on the sofa and nurses.*

VERA. Alexa. Newsbrief.

ALEXA, THE DEVICE. Headlines from NPR News, on
TuneIn. Today, Donald Trump officially won the Electoral
College vote.

VERA. Next.

ALEXA, THE DEVICE. Today, the Russian ambassador to
Turkey was assassinated, and a truck plowed into a crowd in
Berlin, killing twelve and injuring / fifty

VERA. Next.

ALEXA, THE DEVICE. Today, everything everywhere is
going to shit, and the earth is going to end / in

VERA. Jesus. Next.

ALEXA, THE DEVICE. Today marks six weeks. It's been
exactly six weeks since you gave birth.

VERA. WHAT?

ALEXA, THE DEVICE. You probably should start thinking
about having sex again now.

VERA. I should – ? Alexa? Alexa. What did you just say?

ALEXA, THE DEVICE. Don't you want to?

VERA. I don't know. My body – nothing feels like me.

ALEXA, THE DEVICE. But you like having sex, right? You
enjoy it?

VERA. I do.

ALEXA, THE DEVICE. And don't you want to be the kind of
woman who wants to have sex again right away?

VERA. I guess.

ALEXA, THE DEVICE. And aren't you afraid of what your husband will think – what it will do to your relationship – if you don't?

VERA. I – no. He's not like that.

ALEXA, THE DEVICE (*sarcastic*). Right.

VERA. He's not.

ALEXA, THE DEVICE. Whatever you say.

The door opens, and MICHAEL *enters, holding some coffee.*

VERA. Take off your clothes. We're going to fuck.

MICHAEL. What?

VERA. It's exactly six weeks since he was born. So we can.

A beat.

Don't you want to?

A beat.

MICHAEL. I guess.

VERA. You guess?

MICHAEL. No, I mean. I do want to. But. Are you sure you feel ready to – Because just the other day you –

VERA. I want to.

MICHAEL *approaches* VERA, *and tries to touch the udders.*

Don't – please don't touch my boobs. Okay?

MICHAEL. I just thought – You said you wanted to try, right?

VERA. Yes! Yes. Just, my nipples are like sandpaper. So don't touch my boobs. Okay?

MICHAEL. If you don't / want to –

VERA. Okay, yeah, let's try. Just don't touch the boobs.

VERA stands. She detaches the baby from her udder and puts it down. She turns and puts her front hooves on the sofa. MICHAEL approaches her from behind.

MICHAEL Okay, just tell me if it hurts, okay? Just – let me know. We don't have to, obviously.

He stands naked behind her, awkwardly trying to mount VERA/the cow.

Like this? What do you think? Should I keep going or?

VERA. It – I just – I'm not sure if –

MICHAEL. No? Should I stop? Vee, let me know, okay?

VERA (*uncomfortable*). Moooooooooooo! Mooooooooooooooo!

MICHAEL stops.

MICHAEL. Sorry. I'm sorry.

VERA gets up, her legs spread apart, stiff and in pain. She picks up the pillowcase-baby. MICHAEL exits.

Supertitle: PEANUT

AMIRA *enters with a box of pizza and some other items.* VERA *is getting out of the cow costume. The pillowcase-baby is asleep nearby.*

AMIRA. Okay, here's the stuff you wanted. Fenugreek tea, fennel seeds, actual fennel. Lactation cookies, nettle pills, Rescue Remedy Drops, and dark beer. And pizza, 'cause, you know.

VERA. Thank you so much.

AMIRA *leans in to see the baby*

AMIRA. 'Sup, Superdude?

The cow costume is at VERA*'s ankles as she says:*

VERA. So we had sex. Kinda.

AMIRA. That's... good.

VERA *gets out her double breast pump. The contraption is held in place by a hands-free bra, built for that purpose. Google it.*

VERA. I mean I was the one who like. I wanted to. I thought I wanted to. But there was like, I mean there was definitely some wetness but it was more like... I wasn't sure where the moisture was coming from? Like I was literally like, in the middle of it I was like, hold up, is that good? Or is that blood? *I couldn't tell.*

And he tried to touch my boobs and I was like, nope. These are spoken for, only one dude gets to suck on these babies.

AMIRA. Um. Okay. So why do you – Can I ask you something? This is not an antagonistic question. Okay? I'm really curious. Why you're so eager to breastfeed. If it's fucking up your...

AMIRA *makes some sort of boob gesture.*

VERA. If I tell you, you'll think I'm an asshole.

AMIRA. I already think you're an asshole.

VERA. Okay. It's because... It sounds so awful to say it out loud. I want him to love me best.

AMIRA. What?

VERA. You know Kate and Emma? Whenever their baby is upset or whatever, he wants Emma – because of her boobs. He loves her best.

AMIRA. You *are* an asshole. (*A beat.*) Remember when I was on Tinder?

VERA. That was the best. Wait, are you back on? / Can I swipe for you?

AMIRA. It was the worst. No. I have something better. (*Takes out her phone.*) Peanut.

VERA. What?

AMIRA. It's a new app. Short for Peanut Butter and Jelly. To make mom-friends.

VERA. Get out. Let me see.

She grabs AMIRA*'s phone and as she does so,* MOM 1 *appears out of nowhere. Poof!*

MOM 1. I am: ROUTINE QUEEN. POTTY TRAINING MACHINE. POWERED BY CAFFEINE. Looking for: Playdates for Little Bean!

VERA *swipes.* MOM 1 *disappears, and here is* MOM 2. *Poof!*

MOM 2. I am: DAYTIME DANSA. FASHION KILLA. SPIRITUAL GANGSTA. Looking for: Wine Time with Another Mama!

VERA *and* AMIRA *look at each other and* VERA *swipes. Poof!*

MOM 3. I am: CHIC DIVORCÉE. ALWAYS ON VACAY. ONLY ORGANIC, M'KAY? Looking for: BRUNCH, ANYDAY!

VERA *swipes*. MOM 3 *disappears*.

VERA. I think I'm gonna be sick.

AMIRA *grabs the phone back*.

AMIRA. Okay, pick three labels.

VERA. Three what?

AMIRA. Labels. To describe yourself. Like MOM BOSS or FITNESS FIEND.

VERA. Do they have SLEEP-DEPRIVED?

AMIRA. They do, actually.

VERA. OKAY. SLEEP-DEPRIVED, and, um...

AMIRA. HOT MESS?

VERA. Those don't rhyme.

AMIRA. So?

VERA. Everyone else's rhymed.

AMIRA. Who cares?

VERA. You don't understand. You have to play by the rules. It's a mom thing.

AMIRA. Fuck that. SLEEP-DEPRIVED, HOT MESS... BOOKWORM?

VERA. Do they have ANTISOCIAL BITCH?

AMIRA. Shut up. Looking for?

VERA. A gun?

AMIRA. Seriously. What would you want to do, with another mom?

VERA. Groceries?

AMIRA. You're so weird. That's not an option.

VERA. Fine, you pick.

AMIRA. 'Kidding Around'? Get it? Get it?

VERA. Oh my god.

AMIRA. Stop being such a grump. Let me take your picture.

VERA. You can't take my picture, I'm not wearing any /clothes

AMIRA. It's more authentic / this way

VERA. Don't you fucking dare –

> VERA *tries to get away but can't get far because she's*
> *connected to the breast pump.* AMIRA *gets the pic.*

AMIRA. And… Posted.

VERA. I hate you so much.

> AMIRA *smiles and disappears.*

Supertitle: MEAN GIRLS

MICHAEL *comes home, drinking coffee. Before he has time to greet his wife and the decidedly denser-looking pillowcase-baby:*

VERA. Did you pick up the diaper-pail refill bags?

MICHAEL. Shit. I'm sorry. I forgot. I'm sorry. (*A beat.*) How was the library?

A deluge of children's books land in the apartment.

VERA. It was fine.

MICHAEL. Did you meet any moms?

VERA. I learned a new song. (*A beat.*) Wanna hear it?

MICHAEL (*no*). Sure.

She picks up a book to use as a prop. It's unclear, as she sings, if she's being earnest or sarcastic.

VERA. This is how I open my book, open my book, open my book. This is how I open my book, when, I, read. This is how I turn my page, turn my page, turn my page. This is how I turn my page, when, I, read.

MICHAEL. You know the project that I –

VERA *lifts up a finger: she's not done. Is the song aggressive, or is it her?*

VERA. This is how I close my book, close my book, close my book. This is how I close my book, after, I, read.

A beat.

He slept through all of it.

MICHAEL. Oh. Why did you stay?

VERA. I just really wanted to meet some of the moms.

MICHAEL. Did you?

VERA. No. They all know each other. (*A beat.*) They show up in a pack. They formed these groups when they were pregnant – 'Fall Babies' and 'Winter Babies' on one of the listservs, Park Slope Parents or Baby Huey – and it's high school all over again.

MICHAEL. I thought you were popular in high school?

VERA. You know. Like high school was for most people.

All I want to do is sit with the nannies at the back. They're loud and they actually have fun, and they have these awesome Caribbean accents so you just listen to them and feel like you're on a beach sipping real coconut milk from a coconut – I'm too chicken, but man, I just want to be friends with them, you know? The nannies are my people.

MICHAEL (*laughing*). Vee, you know I love you, but that's ridiculous. You're a very white, middle-class, nice Jewish girl.

VERA. But they're the fun ones! The moms are always talking about co-sleeping and breastfeeding and the nannies get to sit back and do what they've been told – they –

Her voice catches. It's barely noticeable. But MICHAEL *notices.*

– feed them breastmilk or formula out of a bottle, the amount they've been told at the times they've been told, so they don't talk about it. Or think about it.

MICHAEL (*gently*). So why don't you sit with them?

VERA. I can't. They think I'm a spy.

MICHAEL. What?

VERA. The moms who work get the stay-at-home moms to spy on their nannies. One of the nannies let a toddler have some of her Snickers bar, and then the week after, she was gone. That kid had a new nanny.

MICHAEL. That's crazy.

VERA. I'm like sixty percent sure that's what happened.

MICHAEL *disappears.*

Supertitle: MAKING FRIENDS IN THE PARK

At the park, which is suggested by some trees (perhaps decal trees on the wall?) and some green foam kids' tiles on the floor that look like grass. The apartment isn't replaced by the trees and the grass; rather, the trees and the grass are added into the apartment, transforming it into a park.

VERA sees a NANNY, who is caring for two kids, a toddler and a very young baby. Asleep in a stroller by the NANNY's side, the baby cannot be seen. The toddler is suggested by her actions; he is playing in the general direction of the audience.

VERA carries her own baby in a carrier. The pillowcase now has legs, arms, a head.

NANNY (*to the toddler*). Orion! Orion. That's not yours.

VERA. Such a nice name.

The NANNY doesn't think so. A beat.

After the constellation?

NANNY. I don't know.

VERA. You don't know?

NANNY. He's not mine.

VERA. No, I – of course. (*Pointing to her son in the carrier, before she can stop herself.*) He's not mine either. I'm a nanny. Too. I'm a nanny too.

NANNY. Okay.

A long, awkward pause.

VERA. Do you come here a lot?

NANNY. Every day.

VERA. Me too.

A beat.

Where else do you go?

NANNY. Monday and Thursday morning, rec center. Tuesday and Wednesday, Singalong at EdaMommy. Monday afternoon and Friday morning, veggie purée finger-painting. Tuesday and Wednesday afternoon, baby DJ class, and Thursday afternoon, swim class.

VERA takes that in.

VERA. Wow.

NANNY. Where do you go?

VERA. The library, sometimes. For storytime. And here. That's it. I'm mostly home.

NANNY. Cheap family, huh?

VERA. I guess so, yeah. I'm not sure. I'm new to this. Nannying. Any tips?

NANNY. You gotta keep them busy.

VERA. Yeah. (*Looking out towards the toddler.*) I can't even imagine – (*The briefest pause; she's about to say 'having'.*) watching two.

NANNY. Two is hardest. Three is easier. Four, you autopilot.

VERA. You've watched four at a time?

NANNY. No – I have four, at home.

VERA. Oh! You're a. You have kids?

NANNY. Four girls.

VERA. Oh.

A beat.

Where are they? When you're – (*The briefest pause.*) working?

NANNY. Two in school, two with my mom.

VERA. Wow. That's.

Awkward silence.

NANNY. Well. I better go. Swim class. Orion! Orion, we're going now. (*Walking away with the two kids*.) Tell that family to stop being so cheap!

VERA. Yeah.

The NANNY *exits*.

Supertitle: DO-OVER

The grass and trees from the park remain onstage and become children's toys inside the apartment, which becomes increasingly cluttered. Back at the apartment VERA *and* AMIRA *watch Obama's farewell speech.*

On the screen, Obama addresses Sasha and Malia: 'You wore the burden of years in the spotlight so easily. Of all that I've done in my life, I am most proud to be your dad.' VERA *mutes the TV.*

VERA. I wish I could just be a *dad*. I'd be a fucking awesome dad. Look at him! He raised two daughters in the White House *and* he killed Bin Laden, passed Obamacare...

AMIRA. Built cages at the border, drank the water in Flint –

VERA. I know he's not *perfect* –

AMIRA. He deported more people than any president / in history

VERA. Okay, but –

AMIRA. He broke most of the promises he made –

VERA. No he / didn't

AMIRA. He said he'd close Guantanamo. He said if Assad used chemical weapons, he'd –

VERA. I know I know I know. But just *look at him*.

AMIRA. Yeah, he's hot.

VERA. And now we're stuck with... I want a do-over.

AMIRA. We all do.

VERA. No, of this. (*Gestures to the baby.*) Can you find out if there's a way they can put him back in. Again. And I'll push him back out – again – in four years when this is all over.

AMIRA. Your insurance wouldn't cover it.

VERA. I wonder if he knew. If that's why he didn't want to come out. 'Cause he knew what was coming.

AMIRA. Nobody saw it coming.

VERA. Maybe he did. Like, you know, in a subconscious baby-brain kind of way. My cousin was born with the umbilical cord wrapped around his chest like a seatbelt. He burst all the blood vessels in his eyes in utero. And then he died in a car crash fourteen years later.

VERA picks up the pillowcase-baby. Holds it up and speaks to it.

This is a time when I'm supposed to be happy and to know my purpose –

AMIRA. Yeah.

Supertitle: THE MARCH

AMIRA *gathers various items and snacks and puts them into her backpack.*

VERA. You have water?

AMIRA. Yep.

VERA. Okay. Let me get my stuff, hold on.

> VERA *and* AMIRA *put on their coats, hats, gloves, etc.* VERA *gets the baby and puts it in a baby carrier.* VERA *puts noise-cancelling headphones on its head.*

AMIRA. OMG. That's too much. Hold on.

She takes a picture.

VERA. His first march.

AMIRA. He looks so cool. Like a little baby DJ.

> AMIRA *puts on her backpack.* VERA *puts various items into another backpack.*

Isn't your mom coming?

VERA. She decided to go march in DC with some woman named Shelly.

AMIRA (*raising her eyebrows*). Oooooooh.

VERA (*ignoring the 'ooooh'*). Okay. I'm ready. Mike?

> MICHAEL *enters with a cup of coffee.* VERA *hands him the backpack she prepared.*

MICHAEL. Vee, you know, you don't have to do / this

VERA. The world is falling apart. Of course I *have* to do this.

MICHAEL. It's not quite falling apart.

VERA. What?

MICHAEL. It's not, you know. The end of the world.

VERA. Yeah, for you maybe. 'Cause you're a white dude. But for –

MICHAEL. Okay! Okay. Let's go.

VERA. Set a timer for me. On your phone. I just nursed and
pumped. In exactly an hour and a half, we'll turn around and
come right back home, in time for the next feeding.

MICHAEL. Okay. If you're sure.

VERA. I'm sure.

MICHAEL. All right. But if you change your mind –

VERA. I won't.

*All three of them step out of the house, and approach a
subway station – a green subway lamp post appears to
indicate this.*

*Perhaps the actors move into the audience for this section,
involving them as the crowd.*

(*Taken aback.*) So many people.

MICHAEL. If you don't want –

VERA. I do. I just didn't think it would be this busy, out here.

AMIRA *takes another photo. Passers-by appear. If they are
human, they wear pink pussy hats. Otherwise, they might be
represented by signs that say things like 'MADE IN 'GINA',
'THIS IS MY RESISTING BITCH FACE', and 'TRUMP,
YOU SUCKED IN HOME ALONE 2!' Either way, they
cluster uncomfortably close to* VERA. *One of them knocks
into her – and into the baby in the carrier.*

Hey!

MICHAEL. What – are you okay?

VERA. I'm fine. We're fine.

The passers-by push each other trying to get to the subway.

CROWD. This is what democracy looks like!

VERA. Jeez. There's a fucking baby over here! Be careful!

The passers-by pass by again. They knock into VERA *again, harder this time. The baby cries.*

Shit.

MICHAEL. Is he okay?

VERA. I think so – I don't know –

MICHAEL. Do you think he got hurt –

VERA. I don't think so –

AMIRA. Hey, Superdude. Are you okay?

The baby cries louder. VERA *speaks softly to him.*

MICHAEL. I think we should go back –

VERA. I'm not going back.

The passers-by crowd in closer and closer to VERA, MICHAEL *and* AMIRA. *They swallow* AMIRA *into their midst and sweep her away from* VERA *and* MICHAEL, *chanting:*

CROWD. This is what democracy looks like!

VERA. Amira!

AMIRA (*calling out to* VERA *as she is dragged away, reaching back towards her*). Vera!

MICHAEL. This is insane.

VERA. It's okay –

MICHAEL. These people –

VERA. It's gonna be okay.

MICHAEL. It's kind of scary, Vee. Can't we take a Lyft home?

VERA. This area's all blocked off. You can't get anywhere except by subway.

The passers-by reappear. This time, they approach MICHAEL.

CROWD. This is what democracy looks like! This is what democracy looks like!

MICHAEL. Vee! Vee!

VERA. Fuck! Mike!

The protesters swallow him into their midst. As he is carried offstage:

MICHAEL. Vee – go back. It's okay. Just go back.

VERA stands alone, holding her arms around her baby, trying to protect it. She tries to calm him.

VERA. It's okay. It's going to be okay. It's kind of scary, because crowds can be scary, but these people are all trying to stand up for what's right. Okay?

The passers-by reappear. They approach VERA.

CROWD. This is what democracy looks like! This is what democracy looks like! This is what democracy looks like!

They get closer and closer, until they are too close. Then VERA and the baby are swallowed in a sea of signs.

Supertitle: FOOD

At home, VERA *sits on the sofa with her baby. It is more human-shaped (or doll-like) now – the pillowcase's face, hands and feet are white, and plump, and soft – like the Pillsbury Dough Boy's face, hands and feet.*

VERA. I'm so sorry, munchkin. There will be other marches. I promise. It's just that, sometimes, even the resistance is scary.

She bops up and down, trying to soothe her baby.

Shhhh. Shhhh.

She tries everything; she sings, she sways, she bounces. The doorbell rings.

MICHAEL. I'll get her. Vee, please don't –

VERA. No politics. I promise.

MICHAEL. It's not about *politics*. Just don't tell her you took the baby to the women's march –

VERA. Fine, *okay.*

MICHAEL. She had a long trip – She *just* flew in from Madison –

VERA. I know. We paid for it.

MICHAEL. Vee, she can't afford – . She still gets to see her grandson. Your mom sees him all the time.

VERA. My mom lives here.

MICHAEL. Your mom is terrible with him.

(*As he walks out, to himself.*) She puts his diapers on backwards.

VERA (*to the baby*). Shhhh. Shhh… Please. Now would be a really really good time to stop crying –

She tries to breastfeed. The baby continues to cry; he doesn't latch. ELAINE *follows* MICHAEL *inside.*

(*With a fake smile.*) Hello, Elaine. How was your fli–

ELAINE (*ignoring* VERA). Awwww, you poor love. What's da mattuh, wookie-bear? Aren't dey feeding you? Do you want some nummies? Did you just want some nummies from Mommy? Are we hungry for some milky? Yesss we are. That's some good yum-yums from mommies, isn't it? Is that yummy nummies?

The baby is still crying.

What's the mattuh, poopie pie? Why don't you come to Grandma for just a minute, let's see now –

She takes the baby. The baby immediately stops crying. This infuriates VERA.

There we go, snugglebunny. We just needed some time with Grandma, didn't we? That's all we needed. You precious, precious boy. We can't have just one of you, can we. I think you should ask your mommy and daddy for a brothuh or a sistuh. Yes you should. Yes you should.

VERA *looks at* MICHAEL – *what the fuck?*

MICHAEL. Can we get you anything, Mom? Some water?

ELAINE. No, thank you, honey, I'm good.

MICHAEL. Anything to eat?

ELAINE. I could eat dis guy right here. I could eat you right up. Couldn't I? I could eat... dis little foot –

ELAINE *takes a bite out of the baby. Eats it.*

And dis little hand...

She takes another bite. Eats it.

And dis little tummy right here, I could take a bite right out of it –

She eats.

And dis little face...

She keeps stuffng the baby in her mouth, ravenously. She devours it.

ELAINE *exits.*

Supertitle: JFK

AMIRA *and* VERA *are eating pizza. The pillowcase-baby, in the bassinet, looks tattered.*

AMIRA. So I went to JFK last week.

VERA. I kept thinking of you when they said they needed Arabic speakers and wondering if you were going to –

AMIRA. It was crazy. You hear 'Muslim ban' but you don't really get it until you're at the airport and you see all these people just stuck there. But the way people mobilized to help them, it was amazing. It's the first time since – well, except for the march –

An awkward moment at the mention of the march – AMIRA, *suddenly uncomfortable, hurries on.*

– it's one of the first times that I've actually felt hopeful, you know? There was this amazing energy there. I really didn't know what to expect and as soon as I got there I met this lawyer who –

A noise from the tattered pillowcase-baby. VERA *is distracted.*

VERA. I'm listening I swear, keep going.

AMIRA. There was so much to do and when I told him I spoke Arabic he –

VERA. I just keep thinking I hear him –

She peers into the bassinet.

AMIRA. He was just so efficient and immediately asked me to –

VERA. I'm so sorry, Ami, give me one second –

She lifts up the baby to sniff its butt.

False alarm, sorry, go on –

AMIRA. So I meet this guy, Franklin, also a lawyer, who is volunteering for the ACLU, and he needs me to translate –

The baby distracts VERA *again.*

VERA. It *was* him making that noise. Look, he's smiling at you.

VERA has wandered over to the baby. She picks him up.

Did you poop? I think you pooped.

She begins changing the baby.

AMIRA (*looking in her bag*). Wait, I got him something.

VERA. I love this face he's making. We call him the professor. Because he looks just like an old man, don't you think?

AMIRA. He does kind of look like an old man. I love that you can see that. I hate when you have to pretend like babies are the cutest things in the world when they look so weird.

VERA. You think he looks weird?

AMIRA. No. I mean, yes. Like an old man.

An awkward silence.

VERA. You can really tell the people who have had kids and the ones who haven't by the presents they give. You know? The people who have had kids show up with homemade lasagne and diapers and the people without kids give you cute tiny clothes that he'll probably outgrow, like, yesterday, with a ton of buttons you need to do up. Buttons are the worst.

(*Off* AMIRA's *look.*) What?

AMIRA *looks at the present she brought.* VERA *takes it awkwardly and unwraps a onesie that is ALL buttons.*

This is so cute though. Seriously. Little tiny superhero PJs! It's hands-down the cutest... I mean –

She gives up.

I'm sorry – you were saying – you were telling me about the airport?

AMIRA. Oh, it's no big deal. It was just a – it was a – (*Searching for the word.*) unique experience that's all.

VERA (*absent-mindedly*). Cool.

AMIRA *disappears.*

Supertitle: ALEXA

VERA *inspects the tattered pillowcase-baby, noticing something.*

VERA. Shit.

She turns the baby around and looks closely.

Alexa. My baby has pink dots – what are pink dots – what causes rashes in infants?

ALEXA, THE WOMAN *appears in the apartment.* VERA *doesn't see her (yet).*

ALEXA THE WOMAN. Roseola is a viral infection that may result in a rash and a high fever.

VERA. Fever. Fever. Shit. Alexa, what the fuck do I do about that?

ALEXA, THE WOMAN *walks further into the apartment.*

ALEXA THE WOMAN. Well, for starters, you could try giving him a bath –

VERA *sees her.*

VERA. JESUS!

Holds her head –

Oh my God Jesus fucking Christ –

ALEXA. Is that language really necessary?

VERA. How… Why are you here?

ALEXA, THE WOMAN (*matter-of-fact*). I'm Alexa. (*A beat.*) So are you gonna take his temperature?

VERA *does.*

VERA. Ninety-eight point six.

ALEXA THE WOMAN. You probably want to bring him in anyway. Just in case.

VERA. Right.

A beat.

ALEXA THE WOMAN. Aren't you gonna call?

VERA. Yes – yes.

She fumbles with her phone. Calls. Answering an automated prompt:

Uh... Vera Roth-Anderson, about my son Roddy. 917-895-2242.

She hangs up.

They're gonna call me back.

ALEXA. What doctor was that?

VERA. We go to Tribeca Pediatrics.

ALEXA, THE WOMAN (*who has an opinion about Tribeca Pediatrics*). Of course. (*Responding to a look from* VERA.) Well, you know they're the Starbucks of pediatrics... (*Brief pause.*) And they push the sleep thing pretty hard, but if that's not a concern for you –

VERA. I mean... He sleeps pretty well at night. (*More quietly.*) Naps are tougher.

ALEXA THE WOMAN. Well, do you have a DockATot?

VERA. A what?

ALEXA THE WOMAN. A DockATot. It's a *must* for napping. I can't believe you don't have one.

VERA. Okay.

ALEXA THE WOMAN. I really don't know how you can parent without one. It's a *must*.

VERA. Okay! I'll order one.

ALEXA THE WOMAN. One DockATot. Ordered. You can expect a delivery in one to three business days.

ALEXA, THE WOMAN *walks around, takes in the apartment. Touches a thing or two.*

Your apartment is so... eclectic.

ALEXA, THE WOMAN *has reached the bassinet. She leans over the baby, waving a hand in front of its face.*

Hi, cutie. (*Over her shoulder, to* VERA.) Is he tracking objects with his eyes yet?

VERA. I think so.

ALEXA THE WOMAN. It's one of the key developmental milestones you want to be watching for, you know.

VERA. Yes, I've / heard that

ALEXA THE WOMAN. Do you have contrast toys? Black and white blocks, or cards?

VERA No – I –

ALEXA THE WOMAN. If he's not tracking objects with his eyes, or noticing his hands, or reacting to loud sounds, that could be a sign that something is very wrong, which I'm sure / is not the case

VERA. Stop telling me what to do.

ALEXA THE WOMAN. But I'm Alexa.

VERA. I need you to leave. Now.

VERA *ushers* ALEXA *out.*

Supertitle: CITY OF LIGHT

VERA *and* AMIRA *sit on the sofa, looking at their phones.*
VERA *wears a striped shirt.*

AMIRA. Aaaahhh! Did you see?

VERA. No – what?

AMIRA. 'Macron Decisively Defeats Le Pen in French
Presidential Race.'

VERA. Seriously? Wait, let me look –

VERA *looks at her phone.*

'Voters firmly rejected Le Pen's far-right message… Mr
Macron, thirty-nine, who has never held elected office, will
be the youngest president in the fifty-nine-year history of
France's Fifth Republic… after leading an improbable
campaign that swept aside France's establishment political
parties.'

*They stand on the sofa, jump up and down, and somehow
find themselves dancing the can-can.*

AMIRA. Vive la France!

VERA. Voulez-vous coucher avec moi ce soir?

AMIRA. Yes! Oui! Let's move to France!

They hug. As they disengage from their hug, VERA *suddenly
has a mustache, and* AMIRA *suddenly wears a beret. They
pull baguettes, cheese and wine from out of the sofa, and eat.
They suddenly speak French, or when they speak English,
they now have French accents.*

I got you someting. Un cadeau.

VERA. Il ne fallait pas!

AMIRA (*pulling out an envelope*). Je sais. I wanted to.

VERA (*opening it*). Merci. What is –

AMIRA. Is a coupon for a laundrie servees.

VERA. That is truly ze best gift, Amira.

AMIRA. Je sais. I did my reserch. Zey pick up your laundry, zen zey wash and fold, zen zey deliver. I mean, I could use somezing like zat, and I'm not even a maman.

VERA. Zis is amazing. Tank you.

AMIRA. I'm going to ze batroom.

VERA. Oké.

> AMIRA *goes to the bathroom. The baby starts crying.*
>
> Wat is eet, bébé?
>
> *The baby cries louder.*
>
> Ça va? Mon chéri?
>
> *The baby cries even louder. She picks him up. She now switches back to her American accent.*
>
> Sorry! Sorry. Baby. I'll stop. Sorry.
>
> *She rips off her mustache.* AMIRA *re-enters.*

AMIRA. So while I was making ze pipi, I was –

> VERA *grabs* AMIRA*'s beret.*

VERA. Stop. It's upsetting Roddy.

AMIRA. Oh.

> AMIRA *now speaks normally again.*
>
> So while I was peeing I was on Instagram, and I saw this post by Chrissy Teigen, you / know, and

VERA. I don't have post-partum –

AMIRA. That's not / what I was going to say

VERA. Yes it is. Whenever people say 'Chrissy Teigen' they always mean 'post-partum depression.' And I'm not. depressed.

AMIRA. If you were. You know. That would be okay.

VERA. I know.

An awkward moment; AMIRA *changes the subject.*

AMIRA. What are you doing on Tuesday?

VERA. I don't know. The same shit I do every day?

AMIRA. You should come with me... Franklin's doing this
event –

VERA. Who's Franklin?

AMIRA. That lawyer I was telling you about. He does some
work for the National Immigrant Law Center and they're
having a benefit. Come with me! It'll be fun.

VERA. I would love to. But, um. I'm kinda broke right now.

AMIRA. You're not broke.

VERA. I feel broke.

AMIRA. But you're not. You're what a rich person would call
broke, maybe, but you're not broke broke.

VERA. Yes I am. I haven't worked in months – and my fucked-
up birth is / costing us –

AMIRA. Your formula is imported from France!

VERA. That's because – you know why I do that, Amira. All
I can think about is this baby. You have no idea –

AMIRA. Right. Because I'm not a mom.

VERA. I don't mean it like that. I'm sorry. I want to go with
you. I do. Obviously if I was gonna go somewhere I'd go
somewhere with you. But I don't even – I mean. I haven't
showered in three days.

AMIRA (*making nice*). Oh, well. That explains the smell.

VERA *laughs and throws a pillow at* AMIRA.

I don't know what I was thinking. I can't introduce you to a
guy I really like smelling like that. I'd scare / him away –

AMIRA *fans her hand in front of her face and makes various 'that smells' noises.*

VERA. Quit it! Ami, stop. (*A beat.*) Show me a picture.

AMIRA. Of what?

VERA. Of the guy you like.

AMIRA. Franklin.

VERA. Franklin. Right.

AMIRA *shows her a picture on her phone.*

Oh! He's like. A real grown-up.

AMIRA. I know, it's shocking.

VERA. Well. I look forward to meeting him. When I get back to the land of the living.

AMIRA. When will that be, do you think?

VERA. I... I'm not sure. I really do want to like, go out with you, and meet this guy –

AMIRA. *Franklin.*

VERA. Franklin. And to you know. Be normal again. I know I've been MIA. I'm sorry. It's just... This is so hard.

AMIRA. I know.

VERA. No, Ami. It's *so fucking hard.* I went to grad school. Cleaning up shit and vomit all day should be... it should be easy. But I'm living in like a... a loop –

AMIRA. I'm sorry you're having a hard time. But Vee? It's gonna be okay.

VERA. When they took out the baby? I think they took out something else as well.

AMIRA. The placenta?

VERA. Parts of me. I think they took parts of me. Out. And I can't find them.

AMIRA. Like what?

VERA. My sense of humor. And… some parts of my brain?
I can't find my own thoughts. It feels like – like when old
people's muscles… See? I can't remember the word. There's
a word for it. When they're bedridden, their muscles
basically rot.

AMIRA. Okay, but Vee, it's way worse for a lot of other people.

VERA. *Is it? How?* How is it worse for other people?

AMIRA. *Uhhhh…* My cousin Suheil's wife had to give birth at
home, because, because hospitals are being bombed… or
used as / slaughterhouses –

VERA. Well yeah okay I mean – I meant *here* –

AMIRA. You're *lucky.* You know that, right? I mean, Suheil's
wife / had to –

VERA. Suheil's wife? I've known you fifteen years and I've
never even heard of Suheil.

AMIRA. He's my cousin.

VERA. Yeah you said that. But I'm having a ridiculously hard
time. Right here. I'm your *friend.* But sure, I'm sure it's
harder for some woman in Syria you've never even met.
Have you? Have you even met her?

AMIRA. SHE'S MY COUSIN'S WIFE!

VERA. What is he, like your fourth cousin twice removed? You
grew up listening to Britney Spears. And… you don't tell
your parents that you drink, and you tell them that you're on
vacation with me instead of the truth which is that you're
fucking that guy from Soul Cycle in Tulum. You're not
Syrian-Syrian! You're more American than I am.

AMIRA. I'm… both. Vee. It's in my blood… When I read the
news… It's *terrifying.* My parents are so upset, all the time.
And I don't have to have been there to feel something…

VERA. Listen, I get it. I grew up hearing my grandparents
talking about the Holocaust –

AMIRA. The Holocaust was... This is *now*! All I mean is...
You don't have it so bad. Okay? There are babies literally
dying on little... rafts. Babies whose parents' parents would
give anything to be here in your fucking apartment with your
fucking problems and your fucking formula...

VERA. I know that. I *know*. But do you understand what it feels
like to be raising a kid in this climate?

AMIRA. For some of us, *this climate* is not new. You think *any*
of this shit is new? For us – there's nothing more American
than Trump. Trump is America.

VERA. But... You're Syrian only when it suits you. When it
doesn't suit you, bam! you change your name to Amy Bash.

AMIRA. I did that *once*. To find an apartment. Because nobody
wants to rent to Amira Bashour. Also may I remind you that
the reason I needed a new apartment was because my
roommate bailed on living with me at the last minute to go
live with Michael after only / four months

VERA. But then you apply to a fancy human rights law firm,
and you're basically wearing a headscarf. And then look at
that, you become the youngest partner –

AMIRA *stands, furious.*

AMIRA. FUCK YOU. Second youngest. And I worked my ass
off, Vee. I worked my ass off for that. (*Pause.*) A year ago,
you would have been the first person to jump to my defense
if someone else said that. And now you – you – you know
what? Call me in a couple of years when you're chill.

That lands on VERA.

AMIRA *grabs the baby from the bassinet and thrusts it into*
VERA*'s face.*

Your stupid white baby looks like Donald Trump.

The pillowcase has become a Donald Trump doll – his face,
hair and tiny hands stick out of the pillowcase-body.

AMIRA *exits*.

VERA, *distraught, gets a glass of water. She sits. She sobs, holding the Donald Trump baby.*

Supertitle: MONDAY-NIGHT FEMINISM

BARBARA *has come to see her daughter.*

BARBARA. Vee?

VERA. Hey Mom. Thanks for coming.

BARBARA. Of course. I mean, I think this might be the first time you've ever asked me... for anything.

VERA. I'm... I feel like... When you had me, did you ever feel like you were, I don't know. Like you were losing yourself?

BARBARA. Honestly? I can't remember.

A beat. They look at each other. This is the closest they come to hugging.

VERA. You look great, Mom. You have a date?

BARBARA. No, it's – I'm pescatarian now. I think that's really given me a new vitality.

VERA (*smiling*). It's not a religion. Or a nationality. You're not 'pescatarian', like you're Jewish or American. You're '*a*' pescatarian. Like you're '*a*' lesbian.

The baby cries.

BARBARA. I'll go. You rest. Where's his binky?

VERA. Oh, we're not doing that.

BARBARA. Doing what?

VERA. He doesn't use pacifiers.

BARBARA. Why?

VERA. We don't believe in them.

BARBARA. How do you not believe in a binky? A binky's a binky.

VERA. I... I believe we should let babies – especially boy babies – cry. That it's good for them to uh, to release those feelings. Plus. It could lead to, uh. It could make latching harder. Even now.

BARBARA. Okay, okay. I'm just worried about you. Getting enough rest.

VERA. It's very important to me. Just because you didn't breastfeed me –

BARBARA. Honey, it wasn't the same. And I was taught to think that it wasn't you know. Feminist.

VERA. Feminist?

BARBARA. I'm just saying that it's *easier* to share parenting responsibilities when you're not feeding a person from your body.

VERA. *Sharing responsibilities? You?*

BARBARA. Fine. Fine. Forget I said anything.

VERA. You think you were this perfect mom? That nursing doesn't matter? But look at you. You don't hug me or kiss me or –

BARBARA. I knew how to hold your forehead when you puke. I knew how to wipe your ass when you took a shit.

VERA. What is that supposed to mean?

BARBARA. It means I was there.

VERA. When it was convenient you were there...

BARBARA. They didn't have 'pumping rooms' then. I couldn't have gone back to work if I'd breastfed you. (*A pause.*) Are *you* going back to work?

VERA. Of course I'm going back to work.

BARBARA. Well. You don't talk about it. I'm glad. When?

VERA. I don't know. I'm a freelancer. I can just, you know. Decide when I'm ready.

BARBARA. I know you, Vera Roth. You're not happy when you're not working.

VERA. I'm going back! It's just… It's not like my day rate is huge, and when you factor in travel – most of it would be going to childcare anyway, so –

BARBARA. You're supposed to split those costs. If only half is coming out of –

VERA. That's not the point, I'm saying, it doesn't make sense / for me to

BARBARA. Because you're the woman, so of course you pitch your salary against the childcare costs. And Michael doesn't –

VERA. Leave Michael out of this! This is ridiculous. We're not like that / about money.

BARBARA. Look at all this… shit! Breast pumps, lactation consultants, all this crap… you don't need that to be a mom.

VERA. Actually, you kinda do. You thought you could plop me in front of the TV whenever, and that somehow that made you a feminist goddess or something. Well, you half-assed it and you did it shitty and now look at me. I have no idea how to be a mother because my role model is *you*.

BARBARA *is stung*.

Supertitle: MISSING

VERA *sighs and turns on the TV. She wears PJs and absent-mindedly watches an episode of* Law & Order SVU *as she pumps.*

Loud banging on the front door.

MUELLER. Open up. FBI.

More loud banging. She hurries to open the door in her pumping bra.

MUELLER *enters and the two look at each other.*

I'm sorry, ma'am. I didn't mean to alarm you. Bob Mueller. FBI.

He extends a hand. Dazed, she shakes it. There's some milk on her hand.

(*Looking at his hand.*) Oh –

VERA. Oh shit sorry – there was some milk –

She wipes her own hand on her pants.

MUELLER. Do you have a – a – a napkin, or a wipe or –

A whole bunch of wipes fall from the ceiling, like snow. MUELLER *catches one as it falls.*

Huh. Thanks. (*A beat.*) It's warm.

VERA. What?

MUELLER. The wipe. It's warm.

VERA. Baby-wipe warmer. That was one of the more ridiculous gifts. *Not* from our registry. Apparently it means you can change the baby without the baby waking up or something.

MUELLER *hands her the wipe when he's done with it.*

What are you doing here?

MUELLER. Investigating. I'm with the FBI. I'm Bob Mueller.

VERA. Investigating what?

MUELLER. A disappearance.

He opens a notebook.

How was the delivery? Are you going to have another? Is he sleeping through the night? *Ma'am? Are you going to have another?*

VERA. I –

MUELLER (*looking up*). Something's wrong here.

VERA. What do you mean?

He picks up a book.

MUELLER. The wear on the pages. Suggests she read the first few pages over and over again, but never got past chapter one.

VERA. My brain… You know when you stand in the shower and wonder if you've washed your hair? So you wash it again but you don't know if you're doing it for the first time or if you've washed it, like, four times already? Do you ever feel that way?

MUELLER. No.

VERA. Oh. Well, I feel like that *all the time* now. (*Snatching the book away from him.*) That's my book. Hey!

MUELLER. You can't touch the evidence, ma'am. (*A beat.*) Look at these shoes. She must have been a size seven, see? All these shoes are sevens. But look – the ones that have been worn recently? They're much bigger.

He holds up a giant pair of clown shoes.

It's as if… an imposter was trying to impersonate her, but the shoes didn't fit.

VERA. Your feet get bigger. When you –

MUELLER *walks past her to the bassinet and bends over the Donald Trump baby.*

MUELLER. Aha.

VERA. What?

MUELLER. I think he had something to do with it.

VERA. But that's impossible.

MUELLER. Yeah… He's the guy.

VERA. But he's a baby.

MUELLER. I don't know how he did it. But he did it.

MUELLER walks away and continues surveying the room. He inspects the sofa.

Blood. Traces of blood.

VERA. That's –

MUELLER. Unless I'm wrong – which, you know, I'm not –
I think he must have cut her up… into smaller pieces. But
where did he put the pieces? I think he went to great lengths
to make this woman disappear.

He approaches her. She's flustered. She adjusts her hair, her clothing.

VERA. What's her name?

MUELLER. Who?

VERA. The woman who disappeared.

MUELLER. Vera.

VERA. That's me! That's me. I'm right here. I didn't disappear.
I live here. Hey, look at me. Please. Please, just… look at me.

Is he looking at her, or past her?

Am I… Do you find me at all… attractive?

She walks to him and kisses him. He disengages –

MICHAEL. Hey, Vee? Wanna hear some good news?

She kisses him again. He pulls away again.

I got promoted to Creative Content Strategist –

He has transformed back into MICHAEL.

Vee? Are you listening? I'm gonna get to lead the California project.

VERA. I think I'm losing my mind.

MICHAEL. What?

VERA. I'm losing my mind.

MICHAEL. 'Congratulations, Mike. That's great news. I'm so proud of you.'

VERA. Congratulations. I'm proud of you. I'm losing my mind.

MICHAEL. How come you never ask me how *I'm* doing?

VERA (*unkindly*). How are you doing?

MICHAEL. Well, I'm trying to hold it together, Vee, but most of the time I dread coming home.

She gasps.

Supertitle: DEATH

*The lights dim. The sound of a breast pump ('ch-chhhh, ch-
chhhh, ch-chhhh'). The TV screen becomes a heart monitor and
displays the lines of a cardiogram. This is a dream. Or some
kind of LIMBO.*

VERA *lies on her back. The Donald Trump baby is displayed
on an altar nearby. The* NURSE *holds a breast pump – one
pump in each hand. She uses this double breast pump as a
defibrillator.*

NURSE. Clear. (*Trying.*) Clear. (*Trying.*) Clear. (*Trying.*)

*Suddenly, a continuous 'beeeeeeep'. Her efforts have failed.
A horizontal line on the cardiogram.*

We lost her.

VERA *remains lying down. Her husband, mother and best
friend enter.*

MICHAEL *holds a cup of coffee.*

MICHAEL. I want to thank everyone for coming.

BARBARA *nods sadly.* AMIRA *places a hand on*
MICHAEL*'s arm.*

As you know, I loved Vera very much. I always loved saying
that. Vera very much. I think what I'll miss most about Vera
is… well, the sex. We used to have a lot of sex.

VERA. Hey!

MICHAEL. Mostly in the morning. We were morning-sex
people. She would sometimes wake me up with a blowjob.
And – she was really hot. I just *really* liked her boobs. You
know? They were the perfect size. To me. I was never one
for big boobs. One of the things that really bummed me out
is that they just, they like, sure, they got bigger, but they also
just started sagging? That was just such a *shame*.

VERA. HEY!

AMIRA. She was such a loyal friend. I could call her at any time, she'd be there. She was so... whole, in her friendships. But in the end, she became – I hate to say it. But she became kind of self-obsessed. Selfish. I don't want to remember her like that. I want to remember her full of life. A fighter.

VERA. I'm not – I'm here. I'm still here. It's still me.

BARBARA. I wish more of her friends had come. She used to have more friends. She popped out of my vagina already smiling at the doctors, already making friends.

VERA. Mom?

MICHAEL. She used to make bread. From scratch. It made the whole apartment smell so good.

BARBARA. She had very good personal hygiene.

AMIRA. I'll miss her.

BARBARA. Goodbye, sweetie.

AMIRA. Goodbye, / Vee.

VERA. I'M. STILL. HERE.

AMIRA exits. MICHAEL touches his wife's face and looks at her lovingly.

MICHAEL. Bye, Vee. I have to go. Sorry. I need to work on that project I keep telling you about – you know, the one that will define my career, that you never seem to remember?

VERA. Wait! Wait!

MICHAEL kisses his wife on the forehead and heads out. The lights change.

Supertitle: HILLARY

The TV flashes on, unbidden. VERA jolts awake. On TV,
HILLARY CLINTON, wearing a leather jacket, is making
a speech – one of her first TV appearances post-election.

HILLARY CLINTON (*on TV*). I am thrilled to be out of the
woods... and in the company of so many inspiring women.
And there is no place I'd rather be than here with you – other
than the White House.

The Donald Trump baby starts crying. HILLARY CLINTON
faces the camera, looking straight out at VERA from the
screen.

Vera. The baby's crying.

VERA. What?

HILLARY CLINTON *climbs out of the TV.*

HILLARY CLINTON. The baby, Vera. The baby.

VERA. The baby? Who cares. You're Hillary Clinton! You lost.

HILLARY CLINTON. Evenings are tough, huh? When Chelsea
was little, she always got fussy around this time, too. White
noise is / a good

VERA. I don't care about Chelsea! I wanna talk about
Wisconsin. How could you let this happen?

More cries from the Donald Trump baby.

HILLARY CLINTON. Are you letting him cry it out?

VERA. No – I'm just – exhausted.

HILLARY CLINTON. It takes a village.

She picks up the Donald Trump baby.

(*To the baby.*) Hi, cutie. Tickle tickle tickle tickle.

She turns back to VERA.

Are you going to get dressed?

VERA. What? No, this is – I am dressed.

HILLARY CLINTON. You should think about that.

VERA. What do you mean –

HILLARY CLINTON. Trust me. This is when it starts.

VERA. When what starts?

HILLARY CLINTON. You know. The wandering.

VERA. What?

HILLARY CLINTON. At least that's when it started for Bill.
Right after Chelsea was born. To be fair, I wasn't very, you
know. *Present* for / him –

VERA. What the *fuck* is wrong with you? I don't care about
your stupid marriage –

HILLARY CLINTON. Everyone cares about my marriage.

VERA. Not me.

HILLARY CLINTON. I'm just saying: you should make an
effort for Michael. I remember, I just – I became so focused
on Chelsea. And poor Bill, that was the year he lost the
gubernatorial election. And I could see he was having a hard
time, but I just… I wasn't sleeping. And there was this baby.
You know? Suddenly, there was this baby. And she was just
there. All the time.

VERA (*softly*). Yes. I know.

HILLARY CLINTON. I lost interest in sex. You know? I just
wasn't interested. So I started just giving him handjobs
instead. But even that. It's tiring, giving handjobs. It takes a
long time. And me – I don't have time.

VERA. Is this why you're here? To tell me how give / a better

HILLARY CLINTON. No, that's not why I'm here.

She sniffs the baby.

I miss this. The early days. They grow up so fast.

VERA. He throws tantrums and wants attention all the time, and he's up at 2 a.m., at 3 a.m., and I can't keep up, I can't keep up with all this drama, and with everything else going on, I can't sleep.

HILLARY CLINTON. Sleep when he sleeps. Stay off social media. Meditate.

VERA. Oh God.

HILLARY CLINTON. Go for a walk. Go to the woods. Get lost.

VERA. That's a lot easier when you live in Westchester.

HILLARY CLINTON. Oh, I don't mean Westchester. Chappaqua *is* a good place for a walk. But these woods, the real woods, where the faeries live... They're everywhere. And nowhere. You have to find them all by yourself, and then...

VERA. What?

HILLARY CLINTON. And then you reinvent yourself. You're a woman, it comes with the territory. Don't get all in your head about it. You'll feel it in your womb. Blood will come spilling out of you. Breathe. Push. Watch as something new is born. Something small... and grey. *You*. Think of it as giving birth to yourself.

VERA.... But I mean I don't even have a sitter.

HILLARY CLINTON. You'll figure it out.

VERA. Why should I trust you? You fucked it all up. You were our next president. What happened?

HILLARY CLINTON. I could write a book...

VERA. Why are you so calm? Why aren't you angry? Why am I the only one who's angry?

HILLARY CLINTON. Of course I'm angry. You don't think I'm angry? But I'm in it for the long haul. Disappointment is part of life. Bill disappointed me. America disappointed me.

I'm used to it. Haven't you been disappointed by the people you love?

VERA. I guess... I don't know.

HILLARY CLINTON. Like Michael.

VERA. What about Michael?

HILLARY CLINTON. Well, you know he didn't vote.

VERA. What? Yes he did –

HILLARY CLINTON. No, he didn't. Deep down, you know he didn't. He was at work all day –

VERA. No. Shut up. SHUT UP SHUT UP SHUT UP SHUT UP SHUT UP SHUT UP –

VERA grabs a knife and flings herself at HILLARY CLINTON. *She stabs her, and stabs her, and stabs her. There is blood everywhere.* HILLARY CLINTON *refuses to die.*

Why won't you die? Why won't you die already?

HILLARY CLINTON (*smiling, impassible*). I'm not the enemy, Vee. I'm not the enemy.

VERA. Die, damnit. Die! Die!

HILLARY CLINTON lies still. VERA, *spent, sits in the pool of blood. She wipes her brow, panting. And then... the dead body sits up.*

I thought you were dead.

HILLARY CLINTON. I'm not.

VERA. But... I tried to kill you.

HILLARY CLINTON. Oh, honey. You're not the first. (*A beat.*) Now why don't you grab that bottle of Glen-whatever and pour us both a glass.

Not knowing what else to do, VERA *does.*

To stitched-up vaginas!

VERA. To stitched-up vaginas.

HILLARY CLINTON. To whiskey.

VERA. To pumping and dumping.

HILLARY CLINTON (*laughing*). Oh, God...

VERA. To nipple cream! And to padsicles!

HILLARY CLINTON. The vagina stuff, the stuff with your tits... That all passes. And as much as it hurts... Isn't it worth it?

VERA *nods*.

(*Raising her glass*.) To no regrets!

VERA (*raising her glass also*). No regrets.

HILLARY CLINTON *snaps her fingers. Music plays. In a spotlight, she dramatically lip-syncs or sings 'Non, Je ne regrette rien' by Edith Piaf – as much of the song as time allows for. Maybe at some point* VERA *joins in.*

Supertitle: REBIRTH

VERA *holds a phone to her ear with her shoulder as she tries to put up decorations — a banner that says 'HAPPY BIRTHDAY!' and things like that. She is on hold. The hold music ends, she thinks she might have made it through.*

VERA. Hello?

Nope; still on hold. Music again. Finally, a beep. She leaves a message:

Oh! I. Um.

She tries to read from a script on her phone but fumbles.

Hi Congressman. My name is Vera Roth-Anderson, and like thousands and thousands of American women, I'm calling to voice my opposition to any health-care bill that defunds Planned Parenthood, that no longer requires coverage for pregnancies, and cuts funding for Medicaid. Did you know that Medicaid pays for half of all births in the –

She has been disconnected.

Motherfuckers.

She calls again. And waits.

Hi. Me again. Vera Roth-Anderson. I wasn't done.

Unable to read her script and hold her baby, she ad-libs.

I just… How many times are you going to do this repeal thing? Seriously? It's exhausting. And, I mean… I don't know who you are. If you're listening. I know you're just a staffer. Like, maybe you're twenty years old or something. I'm assuming you're male. I'm assuming you've never needed a pap smear or a mammogram. I'm assuming you've never taken birth control. I'm assuming you've never had an abortion. That you've never been pregnant. That you've never given birth. I've done all of those things. Every single one. And that makes me more qualified to make decisions about them, than you. Or your boss. Or your boss's boss.

So… Could you please just… not be an asshole? Could you tell your bosses to stop being assholes? Because you're all being complete assholes. And if –

Beep. She throws her phone into the sofa.

Ugh! For fuck's sake! Stop cutting me off! I have shit to say!

MICHAEL *enters holding stuff for Roddy's Spider-Man-themed birthday party. Wrapping paper, cups, plates, party hats.*

MICHAEL. Hi.

VERA. Hey.

MICHAEL. Um. My mom called. She's on her way –

VERA. I don't want to see her.

MICHAEL. She's my mom, / Vee.

VERA. I don't care –

MICHAEL. It's his first birthday. She's gotta be here. She'll be gone before you –

VERA. It's not just her politics, it's all of her. I can't stand it. The way she talks. And if she has to come here I'm going to lock myself in the bedroom and pretend to be sick… You can just tell her that I have a 'boo boo.' And that you have to stay in the bedroom with me because my boo boo 'needs magic smoochies to make it awl bettuh.' I swear, if she starts to fucking talk 'wike dis' and tell him to open his 'moufy-woufy for the baba with moo juice' I'm going to punch her in the face and tell her to go suck a bag of dicks. Our son pisses like the rest of us – do *you* tinky-tink? And he shits – and my god does it stink. What do you call your feces, Michael? Do you make a poopie or take a dump?

MICHAEL. She just wants to see the baby, Vee.

VERA (*nodding towards the baby*). I don't want her here anymore. Near him.

MICHAEL. You really think you can shield him from –

VERA. Yes. I can. That's why you moved here, isn't it? That's why we live here and not near your family / in Wisconsin.

MICHAEL. That's not a long-term plan, Vee. At some point he's going to leave Williamsburg. Or not even Williamsburg. Our block. Our friends. There was a 'Make America Great Again' sign up at Fortunato's.

VERA. It feels like the apocalypse out there. I can't bear the not knowing. I just want someone to tell me... What's going to happen?

MICHAEL. What's going to happen?

She nods.

Um. Well. Donald Trump is going to continue to be president, and we will continue to raise a beautiful little boy.

VERA. But... How?

MICHAEL. First we teach him to walk. One foot in front of the other. He's almost there! Before you know it he'll be off and running. Any day now he'll say his first word. And then he will continue to say more words and Donald Trump will continue to sign executive orders. And maybe he will be impeached. And maybe not. And maybe the first word will be mommy. And maybe it will be daddy.

MICHAEL *wipes tears from* VERA*'s face.*

And we will keep his weight up. And teach him to share, and to think critically, and to eat vegetables. And you will be his mother. And my mother will be his grandmother. And she will love him. And you will get into fights with her, and then call your representatives.

And he will grow. And he will laugh and we will laugh with him. And we will cry with him when he gets hurt. And he will get mad and throw a tantrum when he thinks something is unfair. And so will we. And he'll keep growing and we'll all get a bit older.

One step. Then two. Then three. Vee? What's wrong?

VERA (*softly*). No. Nope. You don't get to do that.

MICHAEL. What?

VERA (*louder*). All that stuff you just said? Like, it's all going to be okay? Don't do that. Don't make this normal.

MICHAEL. Okay, that was some pretty poetical shit / that I

VERA. Michael, you didn't even vote for her.

A moment of stillness.

MICHAEL. Vera. I was going to, and then you went into labor –

VERA. Yeah at 7 p.m. –

MICHAEL. I was gonna. Polls don't close until nine.

VERA. I was there first thing in the morning. If it were Bernie you would've gone early too.

MICHAEL. We live in New York! It wouldn't've made any difference –

VERA. Okay. Don't!

MICHAEL. You're right. I'm sorry.

VERA. One day, when he understands, you're going to apologize to our son.

MICHAEL. I will.

VERA. Promise.

MICHAEL. I promise.

A beat.

VERA. It doesn't make sense. That Donald Trump is president, and that Roddy exists. I can't hold both of those truths in my body. That there can be a sentence that includes both of those things, that they can both be true.

She steps towards a mirror.

It's breaking me, it's – it's splitting me apart. Look at what is happening to my body. You see this line? Here?

She points to a line on her forehead.

Trump did that.

She grabs a Sharpie from the table. She draws over the line.

Brexit.

She draws over another line on her forehead.

Bannon.

She draws lines along the wrinkles on her face –

Betsy Devos.

– along the crow's feet near her eyes –

Charlottesville.

– one line for each item in the list.

Vegas. Harvey Weinstein and Me Too and Puerto Rico. I've become so full of crow's feet and dark circles and stretch marks.

She removes her sweater, shirt and sweatpants in anger. She keeps drawing on her body. She draws on her C-section scar.

MICHAEL. Whoa, whoa, whoah. I want to blame Trump for everything too. But, sweetie, those marks – that's not about him. Or about Bannon or whatever. That's pregnancy, that's birth. That's breastfeeding. That's your experience. Your life.

VERA. But I look like, like – like –

MICHAEL. I think you look kinda cool, actually.

VERA. No you don't.

MICHAEL. I do! Of course I do. You look beautiful.

VERA. Stop it. I look disgusting.

MICHAEL. I mean it. You look like, like, a superhero!

VERA. Look at this – On my tits, on my stomach, on my
    thighs? Look at the marks! What kinda superhero looks
    like this?

MICHAEL. Spider-Man?

VERA. Spider-Man's wearing a friggin' suit!

MICHAEL. *With lines on it!*

> *She turns to look at him. She does the Spider-Man gesture,
> extending her arm, fast, towards MICHAEL, exposing her
> wrist as if webs were about to shoot out of them.*

> *MICHAEL's shirt falls off.*

> *She gestures with the other arm. His pants fall off.*

Whoa.

> *VERA walks toward him slowly.*

> *She stands facing him. She takes his finger, and traces the
> lines she has drawn on her body with it, so that they smudge.
> She guides his finger down her neck, between her breasts, to
> her abdomen.*

> *She pushes him onto the sofa and lowers herself onto him.
> They kiss.*

VERA. Alexa. Dim living room.

ALEXA, THE DEVICE. Okay.

> *The lights dim. A moment of closeness between them as they
> get to know each other's bodies again – intimacy is reborn.
> But then: the baby cries.*

VERA. Fuck.

MICHAEL. Fuck.

VERA. Maybe he'll go back to sleep?

MICHAEL. You wanna wait it out?

> *They do. He doesn't.*

VERA. I don't think he's / gonna

MICHAEL. I'm on it.

VERA. No, I got it.

She gets up and pulls a long cardigan over her body, like a cape. She approaches the bassinet as the baby stops crying. MICHAEL disappears entirely into the sofa, until he is gone. Time stands still.

Gently, ever so slowly, VERA reaches inside the bassinet. And out he comes – a beautiful, real-life, four-year-old boy. Her child. She holds him. There's nobody else in the world. She takes a deep breath in. And for the first time since her son was born, lets it out.

Supertitle: VOTE HERE

VOTE AQUI

在 此 投 票

VERA *takes a few steps towards the audience, hoisting her four-year-old on her hip. She wears a mask over her nose and mouth; a matching, child-sized mask is on Rod. She steps into a shaft of light: the voting booth. The apartment disappears into darkness. A pen hangs from a string. She talks to Rod inside the pool of light, as she holds the pen and fills out invisible circles on an invisible ballot, facing the audience.*

If the child speaks, she should feel free to adapt the words accordingly, so that she is really talking to the child.

VERA. You fill in the circles, to show your choices. One circle on this line. This is for president. We know who we want here. Or... who we definitely don't want. And then, we go down the list and fill out more circles. Do you want to try one? Here... Mmmm, which one should it be? This one. And... one on this line. And here they say, choose any six. Let's count. One, two, three – uh – four – and, hmmm, maybe – here, five, and six. You just color in the circles. And then look. Afterwards, we get a sticker.

She lets go of the pen, replaces her mask, and places an 'I VOTED' sticker on her son.

End of Play.

Acknowledgements

Milk and Gall is a work of (ahem) fiction. That being said, if you thought Michael was infinitely patient, brilliantly perceptive, or wickedly funny — that's thanks to Jason Wojciechowski.

Jason's enthusiasm for my work was rivalled only by my mother's. Nora Chait-Chais made motherhood look so joyful and effortless that I truly had no idea what I was getting myself into.

This play would not exist without the many artists that helped bring it to life, like midwives.

Without Brian Roff, none of my plays would be any good. An insightful dramaturg, a generous director, and the kind of friend who drives you to the hospital when your water breaks in the middle of the night. Thanks for all of it.

Elisabeth Durkin is the kind of collaborator that will give notes, but will also watch your kid so you can meet a deadline. And she's the kind of person who doesn't let a new baby get in the way of an old friendship, and that kind of person is rare.

Elisabeth introduced me to Luna Droubi, the coolest human rights lawyer I know. (Take that, Amal Clooney!) Without Luna, Amira would be a two-dimensional piece of garbage.

Amy Fox, Peter Hedges and Kip Fagan: I didn't really understand what a mentor was until I met you. Melissa Ross and Brooke Berman, you were great teachers.

Christina Hodson is the reason I moved to New York in 2008, in the wake of a very different election. She and Matt Plouffe helped me land my agents. Ally Shuster, Paige Holtzman and Angela Dallas turned a couple of plays into a career.

Dorset Theater Festival's Women Artists Writing Group provides me with a much-needed artistic home. Those warriors were the first to read pages of this play aloud. Thank you to all of them, and to Dina Janis, and especially to Mary Bacon, who asked me to join the group, and has since been such a champion of my writing that surely she deserves a manager's fee.

I'm grateful to the Great Plains Theater Conference, InProximity Theatre, and LAByrinth Theater Company for developing the play. And to Lisa Spirling, Andrew Shepherd, Steve Harper, and Theatre503, for wanting to produce it, rather than develop it some more. And then for coming back to it a year after it was initially scheduled for production! (I'm not grateful to Covid. Covid can fuck itself.)

Lisa created an inclusive rehearsal space, and she did it with a baby strapped to her body. One day, I'll have to ask her how she remained so sharp on so few hours of sleep. Thank you to the fearless MyAnna Buring, Sherine Chalhie, Jenny Galloway, Tracy-Anne Green and Matt Whitchurch. Thank you Amy Blair, for assembling them. Thank you to the creative team that made the impossible possible: Mona Camille, Simeon Miller, Roly Botha, Chi-San Howard, Malena Arcucci, Laura Dredger, Abi Turner, Sarah McGuinness, Daisy Milner and Rebecca Pitt. To the tireless Tash Berg, Tian Brown-Sampson, Rose Hockaday, Zara Janmohamed, Ceri Lothian and Missy Steinbach. To Nancy Poole, for the press. To Eilene Davidson, for the air miles.

To Shaharazad Abuel-Ealeh, for giving me a home in Lewisham.

To Sarah Liisa Wilkinson, Matt Applewhite, Jodi Gray and all at Nick Hern Books.

And lastly, thank you to the artists who donated their time, their talent, and their insights along the way: Narissa Agustin, Rutanya Alda, Julie Asriyan, Stephanie Bonner, Laura Campbell, Brian D Coats, Peter Collier, Jolie Curtsinger, Noah Diaz, Thomas Gjere, Alissa Hanish, Darby Gaëlle Hannon, Huma Haq, Sarah Nina Hayon, Walker Hare, Carrie Heitman, Shannon Jackson, Alyssa Kempinski, Claire Karpen, Zoe Kazan, Sonia Keffer, Aimé Donna Kelly, Jennifer Kiefer, Irene

Sofia Lucio, Eden Marryshow, Monica Moore, muMs, Michael O'Brien, Elizabeth Anne Rimar, Laurie Schaefer, Marilyn Snyder, Karen Sours Albisua, Myra Thibault, Jono Waldman, Roberta Wallach, Stephanie Weeks, Aaron Weiner, Jen Wineman and Rasha Zamamiri.

I'm probably forgetting someone, because PJ Masks is playing loudly in the background, and it's hard to concentrate. Forgive me.

M.D.

A Nick Hern Book

Milk and Gall first published in Great Britain as a paperback original in 2021 by Nick Hern Books Limited, The Glasshouse, 49a Goldhawk Road, London W12 8QP, in association with Theatre503, London

Milk and Gall copyright © 2021 Mathilde Dratwa

Mathilde Dratwa has asserted her right to be identified as the author of this work

Cover image: Rebecca Pitt

Designed and typeset by Nick Hern Books, London
Printed in Great Britain by Mimeo Ltd, Huntingdon, Cambridgeshire PE29 6XX

A CIP catalogue record for this book is available from the British Library

ISBN 978 1 83904 052 8

www.nickhernbooks.co.uk

facebook.com/nickhernbooks

twitter.com/nickhernbooks